Shedding

Shedding

VERENA STEFAN

Translated by Johanna Moore and Beth Weckmueller

DAUGHTERS
Publishing Co., Inc.

NEW YORK

First published in English 1978
Translation copyright © 1978 by Daughters Publishing Co., Inc.
Copyright © 1975 by Verlag Frauenoffensive
First published in Germany under the title Häutungen
All rights reserved

ISBN: 0-913780-22-7
Library of Congress Catalog Card Number: 77-94979

Manufactured in the United States of America

Shedding

Shadow Skin

I come unexpectedly out of winter into the cascade of greening birches. In Berlin, this birch green erupts overnight, yellow-tinged, phosphorescing out of another world. During the usual morning walk to the subway, something appears changed. Not until I am able to relate the onset of numbness back to greening birch trees can I recognize what it is. The first pleasure—the anticipation of perpetual warmth from the sun—lets me breathe freely again and smile. But at second glance, the green strikes my eyes like a neon light:

What did I do last year after the first days of birch greening? Was I even alive between April of last year and March of this? I had forgotten that this kind of green existed. I had not forgotten the sun, nor the cold, nor the longing for warmth, but had forgotten that spring brings with it something more than sun, forgotten that there are birch trees which open their floodgates of green.

Each year I find it disconcerting. In other places anemones crocuses daisies already bloom, forsythia as well, but not here on the streets where I live, on these streets the birches are the first to blossom forth overnight. Time, the past, the uncertain future, the year whizzing past—nothing else reminds me of these things as sharply and as painfully. Seven years in Berlin, every year this birch episode. Two, three years ago the green began to hurt my eyes. I hurry through these interludes. I must try and remember. What else can I hold onto now? This is when my new year begins. In my chronology it is this iridescent green shock which signals that which the calendar shows as New Year's Eve. I am filled with anxiety because I cannot remember the past year.

This birch greening, the energy which flows from it is no everyday event. I cannot live this way every day—young woman suddenly bursts into flames on the street.

Weeks later and again overnight, when the chestnut trees blossom forth like burgeoning candelabra, I have calmed down a bit. Later still, by the time we can sit beneath the towering chestnut tree and drink a beer without feeling chilly, I will have been swept along by the tide of everyday events; soon the first snowfall will come without my even noticing.

On the way home I pass a tavern. Two men and two women are sitting at a table right next to the sidewalk. Noticing me, one of the men is taken aback.

2

He remarks to the others. They turn to stare at me.

I am wearing a long skirt and a sleeveless teeshirt. In one hand I carry a shopping bag which holds three bottles of wine. The man leans over the railing and stares fixedly at me as I approach. Something about this situation alarms me more than usual. The man's expression is not lustful or lewd, but instead quite righteously indignant. As I pass him he says, incensed: Hey baby, what happened to your boobs?

My spine stiffens. The man is twice my size and half drunk besides. The others laugh in agreement. Two steps later I hear the shrill catcall whistling past my ears. From the corner of my eye I see the men's legs and hear, after the whistle: Jesus, what knockers!

I crouch, ready to pounce. And then what? I ready myself to lash out. How to attack? Only five more steps until I can push open the heavy door to the building, rest the shopping bag next to the mailbox, take out the mail, go through the inner courtyard to the side entrance, climb the two flights of stairs, unlock the apartment door, enter the kitchen, open the refrigerator, carefully place the three bottles of wine on the shelf, let the door close and look about the kitchen, arms hanging down at my sides. My breasts hang against my ribcage, warm, sun-filled gourds. Under them, tiny rivulets of sweat had gathered and now dissolve, one drop at a time.

It is noon. In eight hours I have a discussion group meeting; how am I to get through the afternoon? My veins stand out, the blood pulsing dark blue. I have to sit down. To be able to strike back just once instead of having to pile up layer upon layer of indignation within myself! What use is the typewriter now? Let-

3

ters are small dark signs, alien beings which creep about in disarray. I sweep them from the table.

If I proceed from the assumption that it makes sense to do so, I can arrange the letters. I can sit down with them on the floor and select some. I can line them up so that, when other people go through the same process reading them, the letters will yield the sequence:

```
W    H    E                        N
W    I              L    L
T    H    E    D    A              Y
     C         O    M              E
W    H    E                   N
W         O    M         E         N
```

I pile the letters together again. As if lining them up would bring this day nearer! As if the revolt of women were a matter of one day! It is something composed of bits and pieces, put together one by one.

I line up new letters. Meanwhile, in the tavern the man is smugly finishing his beer. Perhaps he is still talking to the others about my breasts, while I sit on the floor and spell.

Before I started going to school, there was a time when I bathed myself in the kitchen. I was given a basin filled with warm water and then left to myself. In the adjoining room my parents' voices disposed of the events of the day one by one. It was during one of these evening hours that the feeling of actually being alive so overwhelmed me that I was unable to stir. For

4

a few seconds I was intensely aware of every fiber, every pore of the skin which enveloped my body. Then in a flash the tingling pores came together again, bonding together to yield a sensation of completeness which was new to me. This is how it must have been when the first human being was created, I thought. This is exactly how she must have felt! From then on I waited every evening for this sensation of being created, waited every evening to be created anew.

There was the pain. Had it finally happened?

It was already my third attempt at being deflowered. In the meantime I was nearly twenty years old. It couldn't go on like this.

The final tribal ritual is planned and decided alone, carried out in isolation. The only directions handed down, cryptic accounts of pain and blood. I hadn't imagined it would be so complicated.

In some way it all related to my body. It was complicated, too. I dragged around its lifeless parts. It did not measure up to standards. It didn't look youthful. It didn't have a good figure.

To me, my body seemed old, my figure outmoded. I hid inside dark shapeless sweaters and skirts. In my dreams I was always "well built," slender, flat-chested, and had no problems fitting into standard sizes.

I knew people who taught me to be aware of my body. I tried to plant the soles of my feet on the ground and to inhale from the top of my head to the tips of my toes, tried to be totally attuned to each present moment in life instead of jumping ahead to the next, tried not to let my thoughts rush through life from one moment to the next, but instead tried to live here and now.

That was a delaying tactic, it laid the foundation. Although occasionally I got the feeling that I could occupy my whole body, I was nonetheless evicted from it piece by piece. The pride I felt at my first bra, my first girdle, my first lipstick! Initiation rites and models moved in on me from all sides.

The yearning for the man of my dreams had gnawed its way into my very marrow. I was spending a lot of time with Ines in those days; she was different. She wasn't going with anybody, she was going with herself. We touched upon that subject once. We were sitting in her little Citröen after school—she was the first in our class to get her driver's license; it was pouring outside. Ines spoke hesitantly. She was afraid she was not normal, she didn't feel attracted to men. Something was wrong with her, she said. It bothered her. No one used the word homosexuality, but a sense of uneasiness lingered.

Ines dared to make the leap. During the summer vacation she took off on her own to hitchhike. We were 16/17 then. Beforehand we went together to buy her first tampons. Just in case, she said. A feeble attempt at protection against rape.

These pioneer days with Ines were short-lived. Something was lacking when I was with her, despite shared thoughts and experiences. I felt unfulfilled. I fended off her peculiar admiration and encroachment. It was embarrassing. After all, Ines was a woman, how could she give my life any meaning, how could she conquer me?

The first time that I seriously thought about being deflowered, I didn't even get as far as an attempt, although I had made up my mind to do so. Love could not eliminate my fear of it. The feelings which I had collected and stored up waiting for a man were enough to alleviate the problem of sexuality. The penis protruded from the male body, alien, unlike anything else. It was not so much the fear of becoming pregnant, but rather that this dangling rank appendage repulsed me. Still, I carefully prepared myself to have intercourse for the first time. I could not remain ignorant forever. Time stood still as I made my way to the doctor's office. The doctor, a woman, gave me a lecture on motherhood and threw me out. In Bern, in 1965, it was still difficult to get the pill. It was a relief to know that for the time being, life would go on as before.

But the problem remained.

By now it was far from being a question of love. Neither did I believe that I would become more mature by doing it. But men would find me acceptable. An experienced man would be best, I thought. I had read enough to be aware of the importance of empathy and patience. A thirty-year-old acquaintance of mine who occasionally confided in me about his love affairs seemed trustworthy enough to join in the venture.

"No. I won't do that!" he exclaimed, jumping up, shocked. "Of course you'll never forget that first man, you know. You might get too attached . . ." I didn't understand him. This time I was really determined. A couple of weeks later, he agreed after all. "Well, all right," he said, succumbing to the momentary urge to have sex. "I suppose you have to get deflowered sooner or later, and I'd rather be the one to do it than some brutal guy . . ." He was attracted to very young, boyish girls. "You don't have to take your clothes off," he said to my relief, as I stood in front of him in my slip and bra. Then he lay on top of me, breathing heavily. He had also cautioned me that I wouldn't be able to "do without," once I had had it. Far away, down in my abdomen, his penis ran up against something which was tightly stretched and would not yield.

I couldn't breathe, couldn't move. I hated having to gasp for air. He tried to run his fingers tenderly through my hair, asked several times whether I was enjoying it. I nodded, knowing he needed reassurance. "You could have moved with me a little bit better," he said when it was over. I couldn't believe my ears. What did he mean? I would have had to invent the motions. Besides, it had all been for nothing. I was not deflowered.

The third time it went on for three nights. After that I stopped bleeding, and it gradually stopped hurting. I was in love. It didn't bother him that I was a virgin. I had to take advantage of this opportunity.

I stood there for a few moments before joining him in bed. The moonlight streaming in through the windows seemed to be a good omen. Should I take *all* my clothes off? Let him worry about that, I decided. Would I measure up to his expectations? Beforehand, in the bathroom, as I ran a comb through my hair one last time and dabbed a few drops of perfume behind my ears, I had shuddered at the thought of my body. Out in public I could smile and draw attention to my slender features, my small hands. But now the issue was hips, breasts, legs. It was impossible to camouflage anything.

For a while we lay side by side, motionless. Where were the other women? The primordial drums were silent. The circle of women had scattered to the four winds, their words at the well had died away, reduced to mere beauty shop gossip (Is your hair naturally curly, or did you get a permanent? No, my natural hair is dull and straight as a board. Yeah, mine too! Now I wish it were straight again). Three hasty kisses had propelled him from my shoulder to my neck to my mouth. The world belonged to me; men would lie at my feet.

"Is it safe today?" he asked.

I hadn't even thought about that. I nodded, counting feverishly. Had I even bothered to make note of my periods these past few months? Never mind, surely nothing would happen the first time.

Cool moistness between my legs. Is that from him or from me? While he sleeps, I slide stealthily to the side, peer at the sheet. The moon, the only thing one can depend on, provides me light. I see dark splotches. It seems to have happened. Yet the pain continues the next night as well. Did it always take so long?

Deeply, breathe deeply all the way down, relax relax, do not hold your breath, breathe rhythmically right down to where the pain is, surely *we* can stand

9

that little bit of pain! said the gynecologist as he did the dilation and curettage after removing my IUD. We certainly can't give you an anaesthetic for this kind of thing, what ever gave you that idea! A little D & C, that's nothing!

And in he plunges, cold metal penetrating the mouth of the cervix, one scrape against the cavern walls—five seconds, ten?

How can women stand a whole abortion without anaesthetics? I feel sick. Once again I can't breathe. Must I always be gasping for air? The gynecologist leisurely tugs off his gloves, straddles the chair at his desk and reaches for the dictaphone: "The patient . . ."

The decision to have an IUD inserted had not been mine alone. It was a decision I arrived at while working on "Frauenhandbuch Nr. 1." Up until then I had been on the pill—for four years. The doctor who had finally given me the prescription pointed out that I was a likely candidate for varicose veins. Every so often I used to go off for a while but basically I kept taking it until one particular evening in Berlin when Samuel had a visitor. "A really dynamite woman is coming over tonight, a terrific comrade," he said. I felt my insides contract. His pronouncement meant that this was a "comrade" well versed in political expertise, otherwise he would not have heralded her arrival in such lofty terms. He would most likely have an animated conversation with her; I would sit back and listen. She wanted to talk to Samuel about the pill and the politics of the pharmaceutical industry.

This time, though, I was not merely an onlooker, as was usually the case in conversations between

Samuel and his friends and acquaintances. I was amazed at how knowledgeable she was, especially since she was not in the medical profession. Together with other women she was working on a book about abortion and contraception, and she told us about a woman whose uterus had totally shriveled up since she had been taking the pill.

"Actually, I've never really paid any attention to my female organs," I said. "I've never really given the matter much thought. But now that I think about it, I wouldn't really mind if my uterus did shrivel up, then I at least wouldn't have to worry . . ."

Samuel rummaged through his file folders. He seemed to be well informed about the "pill problem" (he was interested in the pharmaceutical industry's profits). How come he hadn't talked to me about this? After all, I was the one who was taking the pill.

A few months later I decided to try out the new Copper T. The idea of varicose veins worried me. Ever since I'd been working at the hospital, I'd been having pains in my legs. Samuel was away on vacation, I didn't really discuss it with him very much. The decision was made with the help of the women from "Bread ♀ Roses," with whom I had recently begun working. On the same day I was supposed to have the IUD put in, the rally by women's groups against § 218* was scheduled to take place in Cologne. The two events had happened to fall on the same day. There was a long wait for an appointment at the clinic, and because I didn't want to postpone having the IUD put in, I didn't want to cancel mine.

---

*The federal statute which outlaws abortion.

Samuel was furious. He considered me irresponsible for wanting to fly to Cologne right after. I refused to change my mind. Somehow I couldn't help but get the idea that what he really wanted was to keep me from going to the rally.

Having it put in was painless. Afterwards, while I was sitting having a quick breakfast with Samuel, I started to get cramps in the pelvic area, just like menstruation. My uterus was contracting.

Samuel drove me to the airport, not saying a word. Close to tears, I finally said that whenever I really needed someone, I certainly couldn't depend on him. He said that if I were going to be so unreasonable, he really didn't give a damn what happened to me.

In Cologne the women at the rally took care of me. They wanted to know exactly how it had gone, whether I was in pain. A few hours later the pain subsided, and it didn't bother me at all during the rally.

I could never tell whether the IUD was in the right place. We hadn't found out about self-examination yet. I didn't know where the cervix was, what it looked like, that thing the penis sometimes bumped up against. The vagina—a dark opening. What was behind it? Were there pearls in the depths of this body, coral reefs?

Could a lover's hands bring back to life the lost awareness of one's own body? Wasn't it that which we were seeking during the fleeting hours of a night, the splitsecond of an orgasm / what is an orgasm? To be

12

able to breathe deeply, to once fill every crevice from the shoulder blades to the pelvis, to feel, grow warm, *be*! To unfurl all the folds of the body, to be free from all tension and rigidity.

To become whole.

Could sexuality be the means through which I could piece together the fragments, restore the oneness from head to foot? If, embracing, I could feel the tautness of all muscles and then afterwards savor the release of tension, if, touching another's skin, I could from a distance get in touch with my own, would I then experience sensations which had never surfaced before? Could I *know* another human being? Could I possibly come to know *the nature* of the other's existence?

"You still have quite a way to go," he said. "You didn't have an orgasm."

I froze. How could he presume to know that?

It was the third night we had slept together. It still hurt, there was still blood on the sheet.

"I did," I insisted. "I had one!"

I turn away, cover myself with the protective blanket and think, What business is it of his?

I would practice and practice, somehow I'd manage to get the hang of it.

The woman moving with you in coitus
comes from far away
look at her closely
the woman you lie upon!

behind her gape deserts and abysses.
she has put long stretches of forgetting
behind her, fragments of heart strewn in rubble,
boulders pushed before fresh wounds
her feelings are worn to the bone.
years spent on the icy sheet of your fears
the peaks of emotional poverty rounded so gently
so velvety so pliant.
she bears an ocean
of pent up orgasms inside, which she
will never in a lifetime be able to pour out
time is of the essence, thoughts burn, she is
a cry in the wilderness, the woman
you lie upon
look at her closely!
not this warm body
beneath you
is reality
what you take for reality is only the bat
of an eye, a pause between
many realities before and
after

At eye-level shimmered the finely grained heat-waves of summer. Finished with high school, I was finally on the road. I started out with Ines, though there was nothing much between us anymore. We had gone our separate ways. The years together with my first man had left their mark. He had become the focal point of my thoughts, at the expense of my imagination. Ines found me boring. We soon parted.

With each step, I tried to gain a foothold in the world. I wanted to experience everything, expose myself to everything, let myself be molded. Vulnerable to the point of self-sacrifice, accommodating to the point of destruction, I blindly groped my way southward. The initial fear slowly subsided, but I couldn't shake off a persistent and unmistakeable sense of uneasiness. I wasn't at home in the world, I was a guest. I found myself in alien territory. I had sneaked in, unseen; I had dared to proceed on my own—what would happen when men noticed me?

I kept on smiling. With a mysterious smile I asked for asylum in the world, begged for admittance with downcast eyes, with a voice soft and sweetly obsequious. If I stop smiling and glare or strike back at a man who is pestering me, then I am "bitchy," "brazen"—and imperiled.

I am standing at Wittenbergplatz waiting for the traffic light to turn green. In my left hand I am carrying a shopping bag filled with groceries, in my right a jumbo package of toilet paper. I can sense two men approaching me from behind, and I glance back over my shoulder. Just then the man on my left gets hold of a handful of my hair, which is tinted red and shoulder length; he scrutinizes the strands gliding through his fingers and says to his friend: terrific hair! I whirl around and hit him in the face with the toilet paper, using it as a club to extend my reach. Then drained of strength, knees shaking, I cross the street. My arm is now heavy as lead, I can no longer lift it. The two men follow me, cursing angrily and calling me names for having had the audacity to stand up to them. On the other side of the street I turn around once more, hiss at them to shut up. They would really like to come after me, but it is broad daylight and there are people on the street, the two of them are foreigners. Sitting in the subway, I woefully study my small hands. With them alone, I could not have landed even one blow. An everyday occurrence. The everyday treatment of a woman, second class citizen not only in the third world. I probably have a nicer apartment, more social contacts, better working conditions than most of the foreign workers in West Berlin. But every man—foreign or native—can, regardless of living or working conditions, mistreat me at any time he pleases. Do I have better living conditions simply because I may have a nicer apartment than my oppressor?

At that time I had long hair. I've always been slight, it's always been easy to put an arm around me. It was obvious that I couldn't hitchhike alone, I would have to find another woman if I wanted to come through more or less unscathed. There was no other woman. How could I get to know the world on my own? It was dangerous. To get entangled with a man would mean becoming a participant in his sex life, whatever that might involve. That was just as dangerous. Why couldn't I travel without fear of being molested, why was this direct access to the world closed off to me? At that point I was still inquisitive enough to attempt to experience the world on my own. But later on I realized I could only gain access to the world with the help of middlemen. I made it to Athens without having to have intercourse.

In the youth hostel I finally met up with other women who were traveling alone. A black woman from the U.S. and a woman from India. But I found no one who wanted to go to Northern Europe. Athens in August, waves of heat washing over me. To be able to lose my self in the South, dissolve into a day without end, to end this vacation from the north and begin instead an endless day of perpetual warmth!

This feeling of contentment was short-lived. I was gradually overcome by the fear of not finding anyone with whom I could hitchhike back. It would have been inconceivable for me to go and stand alone beside one of the roads leading out of Athens. Seeing no other way out, I fell in love with a guy who was bumming around the world. With him I traveled all the way across Europe and up to London. I had once spent a few pleasant weeks there with Ines, a summer without entanglements, without fear. This time, the city was closed to me.

I felt myself being swept along through London's streets, but the city itself remained inaccessable. I began searching for people who had already gained access. At Piccadilly Circus I attached myself to an easygoing group and went with them to their house. We drank tea, smoked hash and listened to music. That same evening they left on vacation. I kept edging along the city, constantly losing my sandals.

In the subway—I filled my lungs with the black, tar-like odor, at least that was real—an American commented on the faded blue shirt I was wearing. I smiled, relieved. We made a date for that evening. Changing trains, as he stood on the step shifting his weight from one foot to the other, he suddenly kissed me. I drew back, he chuckled in gleeful anticipation: only kidding, Baby. Watch out for the doors! To

17

spend just one evening in this city with one of them instead of being hassled by all the rest, is that asking too much? I stood there pleading with myself.

"That's hard to believe, a girl on vacation all by herself and not in the mood for it?" one of the men who had given me a ride in Saloniki had said, perturbed. "Are you sure I can't help you out?" I didn't understand why he said that. I didn't want sex. I wanted to see foreign countries.

I had so totally blocked out the expected norms of behavior that I was incapable of realistically judging the actual situation in which I found myself.

The American paid my way into the movie. He bought a bottle of brandy. I was on the pill. We had intended to go eat after the movie. Why don't we go later, he said, why don't we sit down and get to know each other first, huh? He was staying at a hotel. We had a friendly chat. Let's move a little closer together, huh? It's easier to talk. He was fat and pleasantly homely. Never had brandy tasted so good.

I don't want to. Nono, don't be afraid. I'm not gonna do anything. But it's fun to snuggle up close a little, dontcha think? The drops of brandy cling to the roof of my mouth, flow together, then trickle down my throat and explode inside me. I don't want to. Everything has grown heavy and sluggish. My legs are stuck together, I can't move them. I feel his weight upon me, burdensome tons on top of the heavy brandy. He is cursing, I keep throwing up into the wash basin. I hadn't made it to the toilet, now all the golden brandy is in the sink. This has never happened to him before, a girl who vomits. In the subway I keep retching, through barely opened eyes

I see the disgusted look on the face of an English lady sitting across from me. First look right and then left when crossing the street, not like at home. All the doors open and close automatically. At some point I wake up, it is half past two. Dammit, I'd at least like to be able to sleep it off. I grope my way to the bathroom, to wash out my things. I threw up on the faded blue. Afterwards I can't get back into my room, I left the key sticking in the door from the inside. I wander through the building through streaming light empty hallways roving shadows walls doors. In the lobby I curl up on a sofa. A cool early morning breeze wafts in through the open door leading out to the garden. I can't find a blanket, my feet are getting ice cold. It won't be warm for hours. A word is roaming around in my brain. I keep trying to apply it to the preceding evening, but it doesn't fit. The evening oozes out from under it, a puddle of brown. The four letters *rape* drown in it.

A year later I'm driving through Berlin with Dave, whom I've been in love with for a few weeks. We have met by accident, he gives me a ride. I've just come from the ear doctor, I have an abcess and it hurts. It is summer, I am wearing a dress.

On the way we decide we'd like to go to bed with each other and go to his place. A gentle summer breeze wafts through the open window onto my legs as we lie there, our energy

On the way he keeps looking over at my bare knees, finally reaches over, touches them and asks, would I like to come home with him? (don't ever go home with a strange man!—but this is different. I love him!) I nod, we drive to

19

spent. That's how I must have gotten a bladder infection.

his place. Something goes wrong, his penis slips out of me. Dave gets angry. My ear aches (Does that little bit of pain matter, if he wants me!) I try very hard to position myself correctly until he gets his orgasm. A gentle summer breeze wafts through the open window, icy, onto my legs. That's how I must have gotten a bladder infection.

Circumstances do indeed color our perception of things. Love is often nothing but a shock reaction. A reaction to the shock of finding that reality is brutally different than one has imagined. Love can be a means of camouflaging brutality for awhile. Love is often nothing more than layer upon layer of dependencies of every kind, for example the dependency brought about by the need for a man's approval. One layer of love can mask dependencies for a while. Love is perpetually mistaking being desired for being violated.

A man, who is in general a menace, is supposed to be worth loving taken as an individual. A masculine body, which is in general dangerous, is supposed to become desirable taken as an individual. Our every day is filled with such schizophrenia. A woman alone can hardly survive if she is not willing to disown her self. For as long as she has the patronage of one individual man, she need not worry about all the others and the threat they represent.

I was still in love with Dave, lying there in the

hospital with a urinary tract infection. He regretted the fact that we wouldn't be able to go to bed with each other for a while. I did too. I needed him because I didn't have my self.

To have a middleman, a mediator between me and the world. The more audacious and unapproachable he was, the more tightly I wove the strands of our complicity, the more I imagined "freedom and adventure." But he was the one who decided when I could go out with him, he opened and closed the doors to the world. I stood at the window waiting for the return of the solitary, battleweary hero. No matter whether he returned exhausted from work, from union meetings, from football, from too much thinking or suntanned from vacation: I took him in, tended to his needs, gave him strength. Full of inner virtues, layer upon layer. Silent and sensual, sympathetic and compassionate.

"You're not possessive," said Dave. "That's rare in a woman." No practice, no prior history in speaking, no demands. Being able to speak, a mute wish.

A world apart, the calming inner world. The division between internal and external is reestablished daily. The division of labor has penetrated everything, has permeated the very marrow of even the most revolutionary of comrades / what is revolutionary? He is not about to do anything to change this condition, his penis is at stake. Hearth and home are no longer necessary as tokens of this division between the internal and external. The conditioning goes deeper than that.

Women are better people
than men, Dave maintained, they are
more democratic, more humane, more diplomatic
All women are beautiful! He also said:
You must begin the revolution
Left to themselves men will change
nothing. They have too much to do.

Beneath the surface of my skin, new cracks were forming. I noticed them at once, but did nothing about them. I was fascinated yet unsure of what to do, even though I had the feeling that I was about to be ravaged once again.

The first winter in Berlin was long and unusually cold. I arrived laden with a sense of self-awareness, the unmistakeable need to withdraw. I had lost the knack of intercourse, once so painfully acquired. The frenzy of the first love a distant failure, perished in hatred. Never again would I become so deeply involved with another human being! Quite a while back I had given up the idea of marriage. It was "bourgeois."

Into the jungle of the cities, to be in the midst of it all! I resolved never to expose my self to devastation again. Feelings were sentimental . . . no more sentimentality, no more pain. Ines and I agreed that we had become cautious. We were more selective, no longer as generous in bestowing our affection. We wanted to demystify sexuality. It was to be considered a casual matter, no longer the highpoint of an encounter with another person, but rather a superficial means of getting to know one another.

The alarm clock scared me to death every morning. The wash cloth was often frozen solid. Ines was attending the university, she had the ideas. I had the alarm clock. How swiftly we found ourselves growing apart again, our life-styles so different! It took only a few weeks. Ines had imagination, I had a living to earn. My sedentary instinct prevailed. You should get your degree, she said. Three years—that's nothing!

Ines would get up only after I had already stumbled out of the house and raced for the bus. The sun began to warm the basement apartment. Now she could turn on the radio, eat breakfast, get the heat going, straighten up and sit down at the table in front of the window, time to think, time to be productive.

The affair with Nadjenka had her coming and going, had both of them coming and going. She hardly spoke of it. She cloaked herself in an impenetrable layer of you-don't-know-anything-about-it, you-can't-understand-it. She was withdrawn more often than before. Sometimes her face betrayed traces of resignation, bitterness, yet the fire in her eyes blazed all the stronger. Whenever she returned from West Germany, lacerated by a visit to Nadjenka, this fire in her eyes was mixed with anger and despair. She tried to encroach upon Nadjenka's marital terrain, she did not succeed. Through the icy mist surrounding me, I stared at them intently. It really was happening all over again, I couldn't believe my eyes. It was like watching a movie. Everything seemed familiar, their longings pains the madness of it all. I was overcome by nostalgic craving for things far away, it was painful—were feelings still possible? The nights were short, my sleep shallow and troubled. My loneliness became unbearable. In a strange city, lacking the strength to seek people out. The love these two women felt for each other was omnipresent. After the initial shock of finding out that it really was true, it became an accepted fact. I knew the people well.

I thought about the conversation I had had with Nadjenka while still in Bern. I kept looking at her throughout the conversation, not knowing why I was so attracted to her. When she can really laugh, Nadjenka laughs as if in flight. Her long blond hair flies away with her, her teeth outshine the clouds. While we were talking, I felt the brownish skin on her neck leaving an indelible impression within me. Without admitting it to myself I knew that I could lose myself in it—I would not give in to such a notion, not at that time at least! The feeling of being already acquainted with it, of already knowing about it from before, became stronger as time passed.

"It's not your fault that you're white," said Dave. My hands had been the intermediary for our meeting. The good hands of women, they soothe the worries of men, they bring up the children.

Dave had no medical insurance, no money, needed some treatment. I wanted to get to know him. Over at his place I did the same thing I did all day long in the

24

clinic: I restored that which was ailing. Dissipated energy, bruised feelings. Women's great healing power degenerates in the service of inhumane hospitals and exploitative couple relationships based on dependency. I can't remember a man ever brushing the cares from my forehead with a gentle hand as I had done countless times. Even after a full day's work, physically exhausted, I still had a tender hand to caress the forehead of the man saddled with worries and cares.

At first Dave's racism escaped me. For weeks we had our eyes on each other. Sometimes we would joke about going to bed together someday. He was much more in touch with his body than most whites, and was convinced that their sensuality had atrophied. If my sensuality goes too, what would be left? When we finally slept together, I gave him free rein. I would prove to him that the sensuality of this white woman had not withered away.

The old sage had two treatment rooms in a large Spanish style building with an inner courtyard. His hands were endowed with healing powers. Everyone who came to him he massaged thoroughly, taking a long time, until they felt whole again. The treatment couch stood in the smaller of the two rooms. An archway led into the adjacent room, which was empty.

I went to him because I didn't know any other way out. As he massaged me with his warm hands, a lion that belonged to him sat at the other side of the couch. He was an extraordinarily beautiful, powerful animal. His coat and mane brushed against my body throughout the treatment. Afterwards I cradled his head in both hands and stroked it firmly along the sides. Nothing in the world could have disturbed my equilibrium.

Dave was waiting for me outside. Before leaving I wanted to go into the larger room, into which the lion had withdrawn. I wanted to look at him all by myself, without the old man. The lion fascinated me so much that I would have liked nothing better than to take him home with me. The large room was separated from the hallway by a purple curtain. The heavy velvet absorbed all noises, thoughts and feelings, severed every connection with the world outside. The old man sat motionless in the small room, oblivious to his surroundings.

The lion raised his head as I entered the room. Away from the old man he became a savage beast of prey again and tried to attack me as I slowly turned back, panic-stricken. I wanted to cry for help, but the purple curtain smothered the sound in my throat. I kept taking the same step forward without being able to budge.

At that moment a little black kitten padded into the old man's room. She was quite naive, a bit wily, and had an incredibly silken, gleaming coat. I liked her instantly, but in comparison to the lion, she seemed insignificant. When he discovered her, he was immediately distracted, and I could get away. This dream unlike any other haunted me for years. Its presence was sometimes intense, sometimes muted. The lion gradually lost its captivating power. The kitten—that is to say, my sexuality—came to the fore. After I had started to lead a different life, I could remember the lion and comfort him without falling under his spell.

At this time I realized that Nadjenka's fair hair had grazed the periphery of my existence for a long time.

This boundary was crumbling.

I spent the following years in the valley of slumbering women, and once again fed my own heart to a black man and to a white one.

Nadjenka regarded me pensively.

"You love Dave too much," she asserted. "It bothers me that you love him so much."

She was here visiting Ines once again. Ines was still trying to persuade Nadjenka to come live in Berlin. She had already found an apartment and painted it when Nadjenka said no, or rather, made it clear that she had never said yes. She was afraid of clinging too closely to Ines, afraid that she would, in the initial fear of starting out on her own, become too dependent on her.

Curiosity and fascination alone—whether aroused by skin color race nationality one's own or the opposite sex—are not enough to make one act humanely. The pleasure one human being finds in another is not independent from the current social context nor is it separate from historical and cultural origins. From the very first moment of their encounter, individuals share in all of the collective struggles past and present. From the outset the tyranny of whites over blacks, the tyranny of men, white and black, over

27

women, the tyranny of heterosexuals over homosexuals, drive a wedge between them, create a rupture which cannot be mended no matter how hard they may try to pretend they are the only two people in this world. The burden of history, unsurmounted, unremembered, thrusts itself between them. One on one, they fight out collectively conceived battles in highly concentrated form.

Even though blacks may be more in touch with their bodies than many whites, and may, by virtue of this, awaken the long lost sensuality of whites, that does not necessarily mean that it is more enjoyable to sleep with a black man, nor does it even mean that, because of his own oppression, he will treat a woman like a human being. A victim of oppression does not necessarily treat other victims of oppression more humanely. The millenial geneaology in which woman upon woman, head bowed, filled with compassion, bends over a man of stone, is made up of black white yellow brown men and women. *Sexism runs deeper than racism than class struggle.*

"How should I begin? What should I do?"

At the beginning of the development customarily termed "politicization," one that commenced with information from Ines, readings from Marcuse and now from Cleaver and Malcolm X, I sat on Dave's bed and asked; "What should I *do*?"

He glanced up from his book for a second. "Support the Black Panther Party!"

As I approached him, he got up from his desk deep in thought. I had been showering. He had been thinking.

28

"You know, maybe I really don't care that much about other people," he brooded. "But sometimes I do need warmth and a little lubrication." A person who needs warmth and lubrication—what can you say to that?

The need for warmth and lubrication—sex—had become autonomous, isolated from the human being with whom these needs were to be fulfilled. This grasping for warmth and sex (not for warmth and affection) was the same as a grasping at things which were tangible and usable—quite independent of human beings: a book, a hot bath, a walk. When coupled with impatient directives (pull your legs up / open your mouth) and the inability to express one's feelings, the realization of these needs becomes all the more brutal. *A man can always void his emotional vacuity into the vagina of a woman without his perceiving her as a person*, without her essentially being able to defend herself, to escape being dependent on him. Intercourse is the price she pays for security, safety, societal acceptance.

Dave fought against the tyranny of whites over blacks and yet continuously recreated the tyranny of men over women.

"I prefer being with women," said Samuel. "When I look around and see how this society is structured—everything from the unions to the police all the way up to the medical association, nothing but men—it's absolutely disgusting."

29

"Stop it, Samuel!" I interrupt him, "you're starting to sound like a real man-hater!"

"Gee," said Samuel, "I didn't mean it to sound that way."

Earlier on, he never would have come up with the notion of a "society of men." We are discussing the fact that women and men relate to each other in a destructive way, that this destructive behavior nowhere shows itself more ingrained than in their sexuality.

I learned that changes can come about only after sexuality has been suspended for a long time, and only after women learn to love other women and men other men.

When will men begin to talk to other men about their personal lives, begin, when in need of the warmth of another human being, to touch other men? That's where women come in. Women are thrust between men who, if left to themselves, would maul each other. Women talk with women and men. If they prefer the company of other women, they are immediately branded man-haters. Liking women is defined by men as hating men. But it is the men who are the ones who refuse to relate to other men, the ones who act like they hate men.

"You can't really expect me to share my private life with a man!" Samuel said defensively.

Why do they expect that of women?

This societal structure makes Samuel suffer. It makes it difficult for him to be in touch with other people. He doubts himself. This society drives him to despair. He likes being with women. It bothers him that men predominate out in the public sphere. The atmosphere improves as soon as women appear on the scene.

Men's glances assault me, claw their way into the creases of my jeans between my legs as I descend the stairs to the subway. Whistles and clacking tongues cling to me. In the evening all the bruisings of the day under the shower under the skin. Cars slowing down, windows rolled down, skid marks. A lone woman, still an alien, and still up for grabs.

Whether at war or in peace, we exist in a state of emergency.

The master of the world sits opposite me in the subway. Four men on a seat which has room for five, legs sprawled, padded shoulders, hands resting on their knees, fingers spread apart. To my right and my left, male legs, firmly planted. I am sitting close up to myself, knees pressed tightly together. Women are supposed to keep their legs together. They are only supposed to spread them for the total stranger called gynecologist, and for the man with whom woman shares her bed. The rest of the time, legs are supposed to be kept together. The appropriate muscles are to be held tensed all day long. I close my eyes. To cast off this repressive posture! To act as though I could sit *unhassled* with legs relaxed. I ride the subway only with my eyes closed.

Day and night, countless times I am infringed upon. This is not my world. In this world I do not want equality. I do not want to be an equal partner in any man's brutality and degeneracy.

Positive change in human relationships will not come about until women are individually so strong that they will collectively become powerful. "Women are every nation's niggers." This was my battle cry as I set out with Simone de Beauvoir's *Second Sex* and Valerie Solonas' *Manifesto* under my arm. Through experience, I knew the horrors of patriarchal society long before I realized that I lived in a society ruled by capitalist economy. Learning about political economy did nothing to diminish terror or sexism. Although I began to have a new perspective on work and working conditions, demands and consumption, upheavals, wars of liberation, world politics, I myself was treated the same as always.

"You're just like all the rest," said Dave when I told him I was through with him. "You're running away, that's not very emancipated."

Emancipated?

I had been battered. Emancipation, up to now, meant becoming the mirror image of male degeneracy, meant disdainfully renouncing as banal and sentimental my feelings and pains and thoughts.

I must get away from here.

I must first of all reach myself. I had set out to conquer the world, and every step of the way I stumbled over men. I bought a notebook and worked my way through *The Second Sex*. It was finally there, in black and white, something which pertained to me. I was livid. I wanted instantaneous revolution. If men wouldn't concede that, they would just end up embroiled in an inner civil war . . .

How would they then manage to be strong on the outside?

Who created this society that hates women.
Who strung this fear
in liana vines through the streets, so that we
become entangled in them and perish in the night.

Who has the power?
A few capitalists, men say (it's irrelevant,
they say, that these capitalists are men) it's
imperialism, men say, which we must fight.

The first colonization
in the history of mankind was that
of women by men. For thousands of years
we have lived in common ghettos
in exile to this very day.
Our paths prescribed, fenced in. The difference
between the first and the second and the third world
is insignificant.
Here we have access to our kitchens,
our children's sandboxes, department stores,
laundromats, a café and the movies—
and yet during the day
we cannot walk the streets without being annoyed
cannot go alone to the parks, and where
do we eat when we're hungry
at midnight
alone?

Who should have the power?
The working class, men say, the workers.
We live off their labor, they carry our
load, they say. Whose body is used
to promote the coffee the worker drinks
before he goes to work? Who

prepared it, and who gave
birth to and cares for
the worker's children? Whose smile is used
to make the toothpaste I use—for the sake of my
kisses and not my teeth—appealing?
The soap I use to bathe—even it
is borne to market on my sisters' skin.

Rape carries a life sentence—for *me*:
I have to reckon with it for as long as I live.
And I happen to live
in a part of the world where I am not as brutally
violated as my sister in Vietnam.
But I *am* violated: even non-violation
is defined by men. For Vietnam the saying goes:
  this is my rifle (GI holds up M-16)
  this is my gun (puts hand at crotch)
  one is for killing
  the other for fun.
and here the saying is:
  "Ich trinke täglich meinen Jägermeister,
  damit mir die kleinen, spitzen Schreie
  besser gelingen."*
No one will put rats in my vagina,
like they do to my sisters in Chile.
I only hear about that.
Tomorrow it may be different.
The patriarchy plays a variety of games,
but everywhere they are directed
against women and children the old and the weak,
against all who want to live,
rather than just survive.

---

*Advertising slogan for "Jägermeister," a German brandy, in the
magazine *STERN*; it means roughly "I drink my 'Jägermeister' every
day, so that I can make the right noises at the right time."

Battered shadow skin
yet still skin
broken skin
yet it still holds us together somehow.

Others are worse off. Does that mean we're well off?
Others are already killed
are we alive?
So many scars. So little pain.
Not even close to an answer.

"I want to come home with you," I said. Samuel
wanted to drive me home. "If you don't mind."
I debated with myself for a long time.
I am covered with scars, I have shed my old skin
many times.

One of them kissed passionately, madly, so that I
felt teeth, nothing but teeth—
and I kissed passionately, madly.
Another kissed gently and thought anything else
adolescent and immature—
and I kissed gently, mature.
One of them likes my legs together, another spread
and prone, another open and wrapped round his
        back—
and I kept my legs together or spread and prone or
open and wrapped round his back.
One of them wanted to keep going all night, another
could only get it on once—

And I kept going all night long or could only get
it on once.
One of them only wanted copulation, another found
that less important—
and I always copulated or found that less important.
One of them could only fall asleep in his own bed,
another had to turn away, another wanted to
cuddle close—
And I slept only in my bed or turned away
or cuddled close.

I now found myself looking for a human man. At
that time the idea of being alone seemed unbearable.
This fear of being alone was something new to me,
but I didn't take the time to really analyse it.

The further I ventured out into the world, the
older I got, the more I lost touch with my self. My
curiosity and enthusiasm waned. I moved more
timidly than before, felt more constrained. The unpleasant encounters and experiences in the world
outside mushroomed inside me, threatened to tear
me apart. Those were the years when I had to put up
with further injury yet at the same time, unnoticed, I
hoarded more and more of my self.

I was stockpiling my self.

Whenever I loved a man, I was bewildered right
from the very start. I wanted him to approve of me. If
he did, I didn't believe him. I myself loved me less
than before.

Nadjenka was still in West Germany. She couldn't
tear herself away. We had gotten to the point of
kissing each other. There had been no other sexual

relations between us. Our eroticism was more important for mutual understanding, it was just like breathing, essential for existence.

I couldn't imagine myself with any other woman. I wanted a man who would treat me as well as Nadjenka. I wanted at last to find sanctuary in the arms of a man.

I gather up my courage. "I want to come home with you."

The music stops. Berlin is a lunar landscape.

Samuel stares straight ahead. He finally lets out a long, drawn-out yes. I start feeling cold. We're still driving. I see the endless road before me, the road I must take to get to him.

When I met Samuel, I found in him a sincere human being. He radiated warmth and sensuality. I assumed it would be possible for us to meet each other half way. Now his features had hardened, his warmth had vanished. Why am I going with him just the same? I am in love / Am I in love?

I needed to get to know him. I didn't question my clutching at a night spent together. In spite of all the wounds which had left their mark, one part of me was secretly proud that I had finally reached the point of being able to go to bed with a man without making a big deal out of it.

The light in the elevator is very bright. I take a good look at Samuel. He takes a step towards me and kisses me on the mouth. We don't know each other, don't know anything about each other. Our light-heartedness has vanished, left back among the throng of people in a crowded bar. We face each other alone. In a few minutes we will take our clothes

37

off and lie down together in one bed. This kiss cannot belie what we are about to do. We stand there face to face. He puts his hand on my shoulder. I smile up at him. He looks down on me. He puts his arm around me. I lean on him. He pulls me close. I cling to him.

Total silence. Craters open up. The elevator jerks to a halt.

In the apartment Samuel takes me by the hand and says, Come on, let's have another drink. Warily, we look each other over in the neon kitchen light. With whom are we getting involved? It seems we cannot recognize each other. It is an awkward situation for both of us. In his room he lies down on the bed, clasps his hands behind his head and looks at me. He flutters helplessly with clipped feelings.

I begin to close the distance between us. Hesitantly I begin to move, placing one foot in front of the other. My face is smiling. I keep hoping that he will come and meet me half-way after all. I wait for him to make the first move, I don't rush him don't make demands of him give him time. All along the equator around the globe I move steadily towards him as our bodies already start into motion. With practiced hands we undress each other. The signals are getting through. Arms and legs and torso in motion. A surface bombardment of familiar tactics, we stretch, bend, turn, get up, lie back. At last we can close our eyes. Our lips kiss. Searching hands try to do more than merely trace the familiar lines along the body of the opposite gender, try to truly reach the person beneath that surface. We try to laugh, silently try to fabricate a bit of happiness.

From books films and experiences which affirmed

38

that which we know from books and films, we know what she/he wants. We act and react accordingly. We react to her/his knowing what he/she wants. We count on that which we know from books and films and experiences indeed being accurate.

Samuel has made his way to my breasts. They remain lifeless. I still don't love them. How dreadful that pleasure can arise even though I don't love myself, even though love of self and love of another are detached from one another, like talk and love, like work and love, like pleasure and love.

He bows his head, at last he can rest it for a moment. I take him in. Once again I look down on a man's head nestling between my breasts. What is he searching for?

I start running, Samuel disappears, the distance separating us remains the same. Is Samuel a mirage? Is my need to be nurtured a mirage? I would like to put a stop to this at once, would like to move away from him, look him in the eyes, talk to him, fall asleep with him. Is my vagina moist? Is his penis hard? Have all the preparations been made for reuniting the disunited? Vagina-penis has become a surrogate unity, a substitute for all severed relationships.

His penis is moving in my vagina. It slid in smoothly. It doesn't seem to be a long one, my right ovary doesn't hurt. His penis is moving in my vagina even before I can reach Samuel, the one to whom it belongs. My first wave of passion has long since receded, abated. Samuel's face relaxes. It is this damned genital solemnity that I have never been able to comprehend.

The fact that I did not have an orgasm is a topic

studiously avoided, just like the question of what an orgasm actually is. "All this talk about being a sex object! I don't think it's so bad satisfying each other sexually, do you?"

To postpone for a few seconds the icy death, to interrupt the anonymity and alone-ness:

To become flesh.

To be recognized by someone, to get the feeling of really existing as a person, singular and unique:

To become flesh.

We know all the rules. Sometimes, perhaps, contentment drapes the windows. Once more we have been spared. Samuel lifts his head one more time: it really is nicer to fall asleep with somebody. My head nods. My hand strokes his hair: His face rests under my arm. My eyes fill the darkness.

By morning the apparition has vanished. Two comrades, one female and one male, meet again in the kitchen of a commune in Berlin. That which remains: to find out why I did not stay away after that first night, after those first signs that here too, hard labor, perhaps even annihilation awaited me.

I was a woman of average intelligence,
twenty-three years of age,
under the influence of neither alcohol
nor drugs nor tranquilizers.
I was financially independent,

neither married to the man, nor did I
have nor expect a child from him.
There were no extraneous circumstances compelling me
  to write with him a chapter of shared history and even
—against his will—to move into his apartment

That's too complicated for me
You can't take any criticism
Your subjectivity will get you nowhere
You're not at all well
  Those things you write with your friends are shocking
You're driving yourselves further and further
                                        into isolation.

I worry about you
You're getting further and further off the track
Again we are talking about Feminism,
weren't we going to talk about us

          You mean more to me than
                          anything in the world.

  I was a poor sister to myself.
  Many an evening I spent in a bar with loquacious
Marxists, unable to contribute anything to their conversation. I didn't know enough. I didn't have the
courage to ask questions. "So-and-so is another one
of those who was incredibly sensitized by the student
movement . . ."
  The new humanity? I remained a mere listener.
Samuel spent the night with me and then, next morn-

ing, continued his discussions with the sensitized Marxist who came to breakfast.

To love a comrade—despite his membership in a particular faction—did not change my situation in any way. Sometimes he even refused to talk to me. Sometimes he didn't display any affection at all, yet his grey matter became dysfunctional as soon as I broached the subject of the oppression of women—in his brain nothing but a vague concept.

He does not deny that there is such a thing; he is informed. He has a vague idea that women are being terrorized by force and fear. His feelings of collective guilt weigh heavily upon him.

"I don't terrorize women!" he shouts indignantly, when I tell him how I am constantly ogled and harassed. All his intelligence, his powers of abstract reasoning, his great knowledge fail him when we are on this subject. He becomes entangled in a muddle of thoughts and feelings. He is no longer capable of distinguishing between personal situations and circumstances in general. In especially difficult and deplorable cases, he claims that women *want* to be raped. In this way he can get rid of some of his guilt feelings and justify his complacency and lack of concern.

This is the reaction I get when I talk about the situation of women in general. But when I confront him personally, his own misdirected emotions come to the fore. Why don't you wipe that snot right off your nose! is what I hear. Why don't you stop whining! It's not such a big deal.

The terrors of sexuality have long been operating

autonomously. They will persist, in spite of economic upheavals, unless we do something about them.

"I am terribly fond of you."
This first measly concession came the evening before Samuel left on vacation, half a year after we had wordlessly slept with each other for the first time. He could hardly say the words, so exhausted was he from keeping his defenses up. The pending vacation made it easier for him to make such an admission. I had waited patiently, had become cautious, oh so masochistically cautious. The time that I told Dave I loved him, he burst into laughter. "Love, that's something for kids," he said. Even being black did not change that. So Samuel's modest admission touched me and I felt gratified. My investment had paid off at last, my efforts had not gone unnoticed. How often I had been at the point of giving up, dissolved in tears. ("Come on, you act like you're going to die!" he would say.)

What an effect such a sentence has, when it comes from the mouth of an unapproachable man! Once again his sexism appears to be nothing more than a personal problem, one removed from all cultural and political considerations. Woman, filled with compassion, perceives it as mere human frailty. At times like this she almost invariably concludes that she has not yet humanized him adequately, that it is her own personal duty to change masculine behavior, she does not think in terms of a Cultural Revolution.

43

Work at the hospital was so taxing that in our free time—much of which was of course taken up by political activities—Samuel and I just barely managed to organize our daily routine enough to keep our heads above water. Though on the average we had four nights a week booked up, we still felt the need to sit down and read once in a while, the need to see friends, to keep in touch with things; this left us with maybe an hour on the weekend to ourselves— usually spent in intercourse. Whenever we spent a bit of time together in public, we rationed ourselves: we didn't actually relate to each other, we were simply *there* next to each other: out drinking, eating, taking a walk, at the movies. We hardly spoke to each other. We went through the familiar motions, but had neither the time nor the energy to question them or weigh their implications: bewilderment, loss, adjustment.

I used up a lot of energy just keeping my separate lives from falling apart. I had guilt feelings about the plight of the working class. I had guilt feelings about Samuel.

I identified with the women from "Bread ♀ Roses" and with their projects. Ever since that evening when one of the women had come to talk to Samuel about the pill and the pharmaceutical industry, my various lives had become entangled. My work with these women had become much more than just another weekly meeting. When I started working with them on "Frauenhandbuch Nr. 1," I had been out of work for three months, waiting to get my first job at the hospital. I was able to devote all my time to the group.

Not for a long time had I been so intensively, so thoroughly, so integrally involved with something that was not divorced from my self, something that did not engender this sense of estrangement. Now I had finally overcome the feeling which had originated long ago when I was still reading a lot.

I shared my apartment and my sexuality with Samuel. I earned my money at the clinic. I thought, worked, learned and felt at ease with the women of "Bread ♀ Roses." I encountered the women's *issue* through the women themselves; it was not something divorced, removed from them. I was drawn to these women, their radiance, their diverse, distinctive life styles.

At first I would leave Samuel to attend a woman's meeting only to come back again to the life with him. Gradually the emphasis shifted. I came back less and less.

Nadjenka is pregnant. After my tonsilectomy I go to visit her in West Germany. Knees shaking, I walk down the long platform at the train station. She is not here. I walk slowly through the turnstile, put my luggage on a bench. She is not inside the station either. She had missed me among the arriving passengers and had gone to the station master: "She must have been on this train, she has to be here." When I catch sight of her, she is out of breath. Walking has become difficult for her. Her flaxen hair is piled on top of her head, her eyes are bleary. We go for some ice cream. The plush furniture in the café feels sticky in the hot sun. "How would I ever have

45

described you to the station master?" she says, "your face has gotten even thinner, and you are so pale . . ."

My eyes hurt for a moment to see her in that condition. Now she is trapped for good, I think to myself. I don't understand why she wants to have a child. She can't tell me either. I had been there on another visit when she got word from the doctor. "Yes, I am pregnant," she said bruskly, a defiant look on her face, "and I want the child."

My misgivings made not the slightest impression on her.

"Finally something in my life which I am responsible for," she said, "someone to give me a reason to live . . ."

Why don't you come to Berlin? Over the years this wish had lurked beneath the surface—the child would mean it would never come true. "You're right," said Nadjenka, "the child will protect me from you too, protect me from the leap into a new life . . ."

How shocked I was to find out she was a married woman! I had met her as an individual woman, and even after I knew she was married, I could never conceive of her being a married woman. Even when I saw her with her husband, my perception of her remained essentially the same, she didn't suddenly become one half of a couple. Yet, one evening at dinner in a restaurant, I was taken aback: she was sitting not across from *me*, but next to him.

The web of do-you-still-remember and back-when-we-were-engaged intimacies was spun between the plates and bowls on the table. These were meaningless intimacies, yet she unwittingly wove these threads anew time and time again. She never cut through the nexus of the web. She only attempted to unravel individual threads and in the process became more and more entangled.

Nadjenka's territory begins behind the apartment building. Wind is there, sky trees fields and meadows. As always, I look on in amazement as she shows me the paths of her life, her stopping places, secret hideaways, things she cares about. There is a nursery where she goes to get her flowers, animals she knows are running about. Here and there she finds carrots or radishes left behind in the fields and picks them up. I talk about meetings, appointments, about circulating leaflets. She talks about the other women in the building, about circulating questionnaires for a public opinion poll.

I watch her while she pares vegetables. She holds an onion in the palm of her hand. She fingers it for a few moments before peeling and slicing it. How is it that Nadjenka has the time to hold an onion in her hand long enough for the sensation of it to actually leave behind a momentary impression? There are more pressing things, time itself is more pressing, it presses continuously, there is so much to be done.

"I don't use the same board any more for cutting fruits and vegetables," she says interrupting my thoughts. "Once I put my nose to it, you wouldn't believe it, that combination of banana and onion was disgusting."

Is that important? Is it revolutionary? When will the right time have come for learning to savor aromas?

"What is so strange about me?" she asks me on the

street, turning to face me. "Everybody says I don't fit into the mold. Do you think I am different from everybody else too?"

Why do you look at me that way, I cannot help you. My lips, the corners of my mouth trembling; I say, "Yes, you are different, but what it is, I cannot tell. Why does it bother you?"

Can you hear me? Are you bending over the bathtub, washing something? Do you hurt all over again, are you going up against the whole town all alone again? Why don't you seek out other women? "There aren't any!" you maintain. "I wasn't even able to set up a child care co-op."

"What's going on," asks Samuel hesitantly, "what's going on between Nadjenka and you? Did you go to bed with her?"

All I wanted was to lie there quietly and inhale her. To hold on to this warmth which has no other motive than to warm. Then it *is* possible for people to touch each other this way, I thought with amazement. Our hands' only mission to caress belly and hips, back and legs, lingering in every curve and hollow. The covers tented in the ascending warmth. Nadjenka's flaxen hair streaming through the mist. The down on her tanned cheeks seemed lighter as our lips came together and explored the contours of our mouths. The silken palate and mellow membrane melted on our tongues. We stopped in our enraptured exchange of droplets of saliva only long enough to return to nestling in each others' lips.

"Yes and no," I tell Samuel, "it's not like what you think, I can't explain it."

And I add immediately: "The best thing would be if we could all be bisexual."

Samuel takes his pipe out of his mouth. "What are you getting at? I mean, I could never sleep with a man, even the thought of it gives me the creeps. You like women, that I can still understand, but me with a man . . ?"

Did I really want to be bisexual? Wasn't it really my fear of hurting Samuel, of rejecting him, that made me say that? Was it a belief in the utopian idea that bisexuality was a feasible life style, not only a depreciated sexual alternative but a whole new way of life?

"We put such restrictions on each other," I said to him. "The whole time Nadjenka was here visiting she slept alone in my bed, I slept in the next room with you. Our world would have collapsed if I had spent even one night with her and you had to sleep by yourself. It wouldn't have mattered whether we had talked, made love or just lain next to each other—it would have been totally out of the question for us to spend the night together. We two leftists are not that far removed from Nadjenka's marital relationship. We are so tied to each other that I don't dare do such a thing, and Nadjenka's mere presence makes you feel threatened."

"I really prefer being together with women," Samuel says once again.

"Yeah, me too," I reply. "I know what you mean."

"I just hope that won't turn out to be a problem," Samuel says.

I was tired of sexuality.

For me it was a question of rewriting my own

49

falsified history. After a group meeting I always wanted to stay on and continue the discussion. I wanted to press on, thinking differently, living differently, I did not want to have to justify, explain, interpret my actions.

"You're not giving me a chance," says Samuel. "You don't credit me with the ability to change."

Solidarity was the big issue for him now. When had I ever shown solidarity with myself? The strength of women was important to me, not that of men. I was interested in women's anxieties, not those of men. I wanted to figure out in my own mind what would happen if women broke free of men.

These roles have made it impossible for people to recognize each other.

What is the most effective and fastest way to abolish them?

I wanted to find out what it would mean to be alone, what the absence of sexuality, the absence of a steady relationship with any one particular person would mean.

Withdrawal Symptoms

"I am practicing living without you," says Samuel. "Every morning when I get up alone and stand there in the bathroom all alone, I tell myself, I can make it without her."

We did not split up. I simply moved out. Three women, each having shed her former life with a man, decided to share an apartment.

I am optimistic. Surrounded as I am by the women in my group and the women in the apartment, occupied by the work of the group, by new ideas and prospects, the pain of cutting the unbilical ties to Samuel does not surface until later. Now when I curl up in one corner of the bed to sleep, I am convinced that I don't need much more in life than one such quiet corner. Solitude is therapeutic.

Even after moving the separation from Samuel is a

constant struggle waged anew in each verbal encounter. Samuel does not belong to any group. He is lonely, and has neither the desire nor ability to experience loneliness. He is afraid of growing old alone.

While I was moving out, I kept turning around to look back at him. During the first few days I went back several times, and during the first week I spent more nights in Samuel's bed than in my own.

I am giving up an intimacy acquired at great cost. It seems to have become irreplaceable. I am breaking loose from a chapter of shared history. I am on intimate terms with the terrors of the present, but the unknown future harbors unforeseeable dangers. Even though the dissension between us may have become intolerable, the recollection of shared intimacies seems to outweigh the intolerable moments. There seems to be a stronger sense of abandonment outside than inside this intolerable state. I know that Samuel cares for me . . . (He has changed so much! an acquaintance said to me. Now you want to leave him?) My knowing this does not make my decision wrong, but it does make it more difficult to carry out.

Samuel rests his burdened head on his hands.

"We are practicing separation," he says. "You have to keep proving to me that you don't need me, that you can live without me. You don't want to admit that things aren't going well for you. I'm only human too, I can only take so much . . ."

"I'm not trying to prove anything," I counter emphatically. We are trying to reach an understanding. Yet after years of scarcely being able to understand or even recognize each other, years of only leaning on each other, our sole attraction skin to skin, we do not know how to start coming to terms with one another now. After almost three years we have reached the point where we can no longer say things merely for the sake of saying them. We ponder, weigh our words carefully. We are already lugging around too many abortive attempts, we are burdened by too much familiarity.

A great deal is at stake.

Samuel wants to talk so that he can cling to the faint hope that one day I might want to come back to him. He imagines my mind to be in a state of chaos. He wants to find out what is going on inside of me, why I no longer want to share his life.

I did share it right from the very beginning.

Just to be near him I trotted around everywhere with him, from the meeting places and bars in the leftist ghetto to the late showings of wild west films. Samuel did not show the least bit of interest in me. If it had been up to him alone, we would not have spent any time together. As soon as people noticed me, word got around that Samuel had a new girlfriend. Look! a shadow which regularly and unfailingly accompanies him wherever he goes. How odd to see Samuel with the same woman month after month! I moved into his circle, leaving my old one behind.

I want to talk in order to gain acceptance of my new ideas.

I am just beginning to live them, I do not have much to report as yet. Exasperated, I want to rid him of the idea that "doing only feminist stuff" is trivial. His facility with words impedes me. I hear a torrent of didactics in a language which will never be adequate for my purposes.

I begin to talk while Samuel expectantly draws on his pipe. There is a sentence imprinted on my mind—you talk so slowly that by the time you've finished I've already forgotten where you started!—but no matter how I speak, hesitantly or fluently, whether I use my own words or the inadequate leftist jargon, as I offer explanation after explanation trying to clarify, as I send message after message trying to explain my new life, my words do not get through to him, they get lost somewhere before reaching his ears.

I lead a different life, speak another language. Even if I knew how to translate it, I would not be interested in expending my energies this way. I find that we have nothing more in common. My need to fabricate something seems to be waning. I keep trying to explain only because I am dealing with a chapter in my life which was spent with Samuel. Was it all for nothing? I would like to know what we actually accomplished in the past three years, what I was trying to achieve.

"I don't know what you want," I often hear. It is true that at some point I started becoming more and more withdrawn. I led a private life hidden from the view of men. It was my reaction to the fact that they did not perceive me as a person.

I still needed a man's approval to verify my existence as a unique person, as one distinguishable from others. I had rarely had a relationship with a man without going to bed with him. Intercourse had always been important for gaining men's approval.

I watched silently and stored everything I saw and experienced inside myself. That was before I could put into words the things that offended me, the things that tore me apart. I dissolved into tears every time I struggled to make myself understood. Gradually I began to recognize the facts and situations that I did *not* like.

When I finally opened my mouth the patterns were there in my mind: Of all the things I learned to express, the most difficult was the word *no*.

It's predecessors had been:

Actually . . . I didn't

you know, I think that

I merely meant to say

what I meant was

do you understand what I mean?

Samuel recognizes that he is no longer the most important thing in my life. This gives him a mental block.

"I am not trying to prove anything," I repeat. "My life has changed. I can live without you. In my head certain patterns have disintegrated, and in yours they are still intact."

Changes really are taking place *here and now*, we do not have to wait for 'day x.' We are alarmed to see a *private* upheaval taking place. We do not believe in this, we do not want that, it is tedious and unpleasant. It is easier to talk about how difficult it is to bring about such private upheavals than it is to find oneself in the throes of one which had been contemplated. It is easier to support upheavals which take place far removed from your own life sphere than it is to leave your own shell, easier to be affected by struggles far removed from one's own self than it is to start from where one is personally affected. Even the leftists have relegated the personal sphere to a position of secondary importance.

"Are you happier now?" asks Samuel. "Was it really so awful when we were together? What was so awful and if it was so awful, then why did you stay?"

Six months before that I had returned from a two week vacation spent in Italy with two women from "Bread ♀ Roses." I had never yet gone on vacation with Samuel. The separate vacations—really a vacation from couplehood—served as a shaky bulwark against exclusivity. It was a faint reminder of the fact that we still did not know how to regard our life together. We had become lethargic, virtually paralyzed.

For a long time now we had been stuck in the same groove, moving on parallel tracks, leaning up against each other. Once Samuel started openly acknowledging our relationship, we did have good times together. We said we loved each other more often than we had in the past. We exhibited our affection for each other in public, it no longer embarrassed him. A difficult man had turned into a pleasant person. His friends were amazed. But in the meantime I had begun asking for more than affection and sex. Sexuality was now only a relic of the past. I had expended all my emotions. Love crumbled and fell to the ground, leaving a trail behind me, the last traces from the old world. Men no longer commanded my loyalty.

The days in Italy were filled with work. In our initial shyness we talked little about our personal lives, and yet a certain sense of well-being prevailed. I read *The Dialectic of Sex*. My head was bursting with new impulses and ideas when we arrived in Berlin. Samuel picked us up at the train station. I stood on the sidewalk and watched absently as he got out of the car. Then we smilingly approached each other and embraced. This is the man you know so well, I thought to myself, pressing my face against his rough cheek. The ground beneath me opened up.

This sense that my place was with him, on what was it really based? Why was it becoming increasingly difficult to reconcile this feeling with my sense of attachment to these women?

I was in the process of relocating myself, I wanted to lift my shoes from the groove in the track next to his. When I noticed that they'd taken root I slipped out of them and, barefoot, went on. For a long time Samuel kept standing there next to my empty shoes. He could not see which way I had turned, where I was headed, what I so fervently sought.

A comrade, a woman with whom he was working on a project, was staying with us for a few days. As soon as he got home from work they would sit down together to talk. I wanted to speak to him about my vacation, about why I felt more at home with these two women than I did living here with him, wanted to talk about what we had accomplished, what we had thought, things we had figured out. I would have been able to talk about it in the first days after I got back from vacation. For two weeks I had been able to behave differently; I felt refreshed enough to penetrate the silence between Samuel and myself.

It was not long before I had a relapse. I could not compete with the verbose exchanges between him and the other woman. She seemed able to hold her own in conversations with him. I was still trying to measure up to his erudition, his intellect. My interests were supposed to come up to his standards. A week later, he finally found time for me, but by then the words had left me. I assumed that he considered my experiences insignificant. He felt threatened. He refused to read *The Dialectic of Sex*. "Why can't you just tell me what's in it that is so important?" he asked. "I don't understand how you can just plunk down a couple of books about all your problems and expect me to read them!"

I was furious. Didn't he always read up on every other important political issue, analyzing and discussing these ideas with his comrades, men and women whose opinions he valued? Why did he refuse to expend time and energy, ideas and notes, paper and pencil, when the women's issue was at stake?

To this day he refuses to read even a single line written by a feminist. Although it had affected his personal life and left its mark on him, he will not deal with this issue on an analytical level. "I don't have the time," he insists. "I can't possibly get involved in everything." "Just *tell* me what's in the book, why don't you tell me a nice bedtime story!"

Late one evening he left with this other woman to get some information from a friend. They did not ask me whether I wanted to come along. It was evident that I, as Samuel's girlfriend, had as usual only taken up space without contributing anything to the conversation. I was the one who shared his bed. Speaking, thinking, discussing, researching, those things he shared with others. The old barrier had not been lifted. Our physical communication did not facilitate a deeper understanding of each other; it was the only means we had of relating at all. The retreat into eroticism and sexuality which stemmed from the inability to communicate and the fear of expressing one's feelings, resulted in a sexual relationship which was just as mute and devoid of emotion. My importance to him did not lie in conversations and common interests which had to do with topics and events outside our private sphere; it lay instead in the formless folds and corners of shelter and intimacy. It was enough that I was present: a fixture in his life as well as in his room.

I could not fall asleep, even the vodka did not help. The longer I thought about what I meant to Samuel, the more upset and desperate I became. When he finally returned I was wide awake and totally exhausted. I started to cry when he asked what was wrong with me. He was startled and concerned. "There isn't anything going on between me and her," he said in an attempt to calm me down. He thought I was jealous for sexual reasons, and when I denied that he refused to believe me.

I found the term jealousy banal like all the rest of those terms for emotion and sexuality. I could not use this term without first re-examining and redefining it. It would not have mattered to me if Samuel had slept with another woman—which was an attitude he found disconcerting. But I became incensed when before my very eyes he engaged in verbal intercourse with another woman, totally excluding me.

"Don't be upset, that doesn't mean a thing," he assured me. "You know *how much I care for you.*"

These words no longer compensate.

Intercourse is no longer a substitute for understanding.

The sanctity of nocturnal emotions makes me impatient.

I care so much for you
you've got to believe me
you are so important to me
you must know that
I need you
only with you—
Orphans' talk.

This painfully contorted, wounded look used to get to me; now it no longer evokes a response. This damned genital solemnity erupts again in all its inner fury. This deadly weighty coupling! Everything that is lacking during the day is converted at night into gravely serious actions and embryonic phrases. The nocturnal phrases are so ponderous that they carry over into the coming day, resulting in an amorphous sense of obligation.

How many years can this same scene be played, countless variations on the same theme? How can it be played throughout a lifetime? Does this confusion and inner strife at some point, unnoticed, deaden the senses until there is no longer the chance nor the strength to revolt?

My feelings were all used up. I was irritated and angry. Only when I had demands with which to con-

60

front Samuel was I able to make my move. Had I given up during the long period when it all seemed unbearable, I would only have been sentencing myself to impotence.

Should I move out, or shouldn't I? I spent most of the autumn and winter looking for an apartment. An apartment for three women. All the doors open on to one hallway. Our paths cross on the way from our rooms to the bathroom, to the kitchen, to the front door. The hallway bears the traces of three women whose lives intersect. The patterns soon become labyrinthian. The apartment was jammed to the rafters with us. Their former lives still make demands on each of them. Will the apartment be big enough?

"I am no longer a part of your life," Samuel's voice penetrates the silence. He cannot understand the new way in which he exists for me now. I regard him pensively. "You're one of my best friends," I hear myself say. This he can't stand. He does not want to be just a good friend. After all those years, including those before our life together, years in which feelings proved deceptive, love proved undefinable, sexuality proved futile, after all those years during which feelings, love and sexuality did not help us to relate to each other as human beings, after all that time Samuel still insists upon that illusive notion of being more-than-just-a-good-friend. Now, when the time has come for a determined and thorough examination of addiction as well as dedication to work, of exclusivity as well as loneliness!

The poster on the wall of our living room visibly upsets him. Two women are pictured. One of them says: some of my best friends are men, and the other retorts: yes, but would you want your sister to marry one?

Samuel has lost his sense of direction. Now he needs me as never before. He can't make it on his own. My behavior seems to have rubbed off on him. He doesn't quite know what to do with his new feelings and needs, he has become unsure about how to handle his penis. He has learned that there is more to sexuality than copulation. He still can't accept the idea. He talks about "oral and manual satisfaction" as if referring to something dirty which one squeamishly holds at a distance. He does not talk of lips and fingertips. He does not want to accept the fact that copulation has to be put aside for a time if it is to be experienced anew and given a different priority. "I can't do without it!" he claims.

Without a vagina? Without a woman? Without people?

If I could look into his eyes *just to look into his eyes*!

If I could caress him *just to caress him*!

If I could kiss him *just to kiss him*!

If I could trace the lines of his body *just to trace the lines of his body*!

If he could lie with me *just to lie with me*!

If we would meet, in order to encounter each other,

If we would want to see each other, in order to find each other,

What a revolution!

Down with copulation!

But

Whether I look into his eyes, caress or kiss him, our

hands fail to meet, they touch only emptiness. The glances splinter the moment they meet.

Blind deaf and dumb, babbling we seek a way out of the labyrinth, we cling to each other's lips. Sucking, that we know. Blindly the penis gropes its way into the vagina. Up until this one half hour at midnight we are separated from each other, we have hardly anything in common. That is why this common orgasm is so urgent. It makes us feel that we belong to each other, that many things unite us.

Orgasm has been blown up out of proportion. It has flattened sexuality. It is all that remains of sexuality. Everything else is forgotten including the question of what an orgasm actually is, and what significance it might have for human understanding.

All those sleepless nights have made me vigilant.

I watch the person next to me, watch myself, watch him and me during intercourse.

A body has skin and hair, folds and flesh, curves and planes. I can lift my hand and place it on the body of the person next to me. I can rest it there. It turns to stone when I think about what effect it can have on the other body. These predictable reactions make my eyes grow heavy. I am getting tired, dead tired. I curl up, cradle myself in my arms.

Now

if only I could lean on you, if you would warm me so that I could tranquilly fall asleep. I hope for dreams. The penis intervenes. Lately it has been slipping out of my vagina more often than usual. I am no longer making an effort to hold it in. In my dreams of late, planes are crashing. Planes which have just taken off fall from the sky, the gangway pushed up to the door does not fit, it slides off, the passengers cannot board. Flying has become difficult.

"Why don't you feel like it? Just having an erection is enough to give me a guilty conscience!" Samuel feels rejected. The words ring in my ears. Between my legs everything is calm and dry. The copper T has been resting in my uterus for almost a year and a half. Ever since I got it I have been bleeding more heavily, every month it lasts a week, just like when I started thirteen years ago.

"Why do you want to have it removed?" the gynecologist asks. "Do you have a *particular* reason, more *serious side effects* than . . ."

"I don't want to be bothered!" I interrupt him, beads of sweat collect on my nose. "And I insist that you make note of that in my medical record!"

"But of course," he retorts sarcastically. "The patient claims that . . ."

Intercourse, as learned and practiced, is an undertaking too inconsequential to create happiness, to learn something about the other person and oneself, to communicate with each other. An act of desperation.

I push it aside. I am withdrawing from the drug of sexuality. For nine years I've been hooked on it. Desperate dependence on this one accepted kind of sexual behavior!

My eyes are fixed on my self. The lower half of my body is beginning to adhere to the upper half.

If I use contraceptives, I get sicker than I already am. In order to be able to sleep with a man, I have to become a *patient*. Contraception has become an insolvable problem. My self is more important to me than union with a penis.

I am permeated with my self.

Whenever I see Samuel, his bullheadedness and blasé attitude infuriate me. He is worried about my development. His world, the world of thoughts, manifests itself differently to him than to me . . .

He prophesies and prognasticates like an oracle. My ideas make him fidgety. He still hasn't learned to listen. He still mistakes feminist literature for bedtime stories.

I find I can tell him less and less about my new life. With arms outstretched he sits before me, staring at me from across the table, convinced he is facing the woman he "knows." But it is *me* who is sitting there.

Will he ever try to energize the imprint I've made upon him, will he ever try to act on his own? Will he do more than merely react differently toward women? Will he make that special effort needed to bring about real change? Will he expose himself to being alone in order to examine dependency from the outside? Will he take the time and effort to discover that leading one single life differently is important for radically changing society as a whole, one single life led long before "day x" (what is "day x"?), one single life which may not bring this day about, but which could bring it closer? Will he reflect upon how far one life led differently can expand before one goes mad, the feeling of suffocation in the subways, the screams in the streets?

Men wear their hair long, wear colored under-wear, jewelry and platform shoes. They use sprays and cologne. The various companies try to peddle to men the wares which used to be intended for women. The roles are left untouched. Nothing more than imitation. After we leave them, men lament. They do not want to have to be dependent on other men, not even on the ones some of us women have influenced. They want the real thing, the original, the source.

Samuel must take himself in hand. I am no longer there to counterbalance his learned, masculine be-havior. Until he can be alone, until he can initiate a humane relationship with another man, he will al-ways demand more of me than I of him, and his demands will be based upon emotions and sexuality.

I will no longer provide a man shelter.

It was ghastly. The last words between us on the telephone. We cannot resolve things humanely. Where should we find such humaneness? Where does this idea come from, this idea that in the private sphere at least—and here again we separate the pri-vate from the societal—we ought to be able to solve problems in a humane manner?

Cutting the umbilical cord took a long time.

The couple structure proved to be a monolith, solid and impregnable. I wanted to rid myself, once and for all, of this obsession with being half a couple. This meant capturing one's own shadow, crawling into another skin, first shedding the old skin—it would not come off by itself.

The imprint seems indelible. To try to erase it one would have to counteract the brainwashing.

One would have to go through a period of withdrawal.

I have no peace of mind anymore. The entire fabric of love and passion and partnership, of sexuality and emotion and personal happiness has become brittle right down to the last fiber. I stop thinking and living in terms of pairs—no matter which sex. Security, safety and social acceptance crumble. I tear down my own dwelling in order to be free. It had been my home for many years. The wind already whistles through the slats, the wind of an unfamiliar emptiness, of a room where the game is played without rules, a room without old, without new people, a room sparsely populated by fabulous creatures who want to become new human beings.

Sometimes I become aware of something akin to sexual needs, occasionally an orgasm in my dreams. But if I think about whom to approach with these needs, I cannot decide. Do I have sexual needs? What are sexual needs? If they do exist, how can they be lived?

If a man is around, it is easier for woman to pretend that sexuality is livable in this society. Men have learned to channel their needs into genital activities, to satisfy them in quick coitus. Thus have they defined satisfaction. Women have played along. This has not undermined existing interpersonal relationships, it has instead strengthened them. The process of degeneration furthered. Penis and vagina are still called penis and vagina, and sexuality, because it continues to be a sphere detached from our lives, still goes under its own name.

Fenna is tearing at a paper napkin. It is evening and we are sitting on the terrace in front of the restaurant "Kastanie."

"Could you imagine loving a woman?" she asks and glances up.

"Yes," I answer and give a surprised laugh. "You for instance!" A chain of colored glass beads encircles her neck, she wears them only in summer. I have to laugh again, amazed by this simple question and the ease with which I answered.

Fenna lays the shredded napkin aside. "Oh come on!" she says skeptically, summer lightning flashing through her eyes.

The woman we had been sitting with comes back from the telephone. We talk about other things. The sense of amazement persists. For the time being that is as far as it goes. We are not in love. We know only that we want to have something to *do* with each other. With this in mind the months pass into winter.

On the evening of my last day working in the hospital, the first thing I do is to banish the alarm clock from my room. From now on I will decide when to get up. I will get more than five hours sleep. My eyes will not be constantly inflamed. I am coming out of my slumber. My thoughts are turning cartwheels.

The autumn winds whip through our apartment. An invasion of catastrophes. The apartment is ready to burst. The first attempt at a new life is called off after less than a year. Three women with their men, no-longer-with-men, still-with-men, also-with-women, only-with-women, maternal impulses and one child are faced with a heap of rubble. Yet another project come to naught at the hands of its initiators. In spite of all the plans proposals suggestions slogans, reality won out. What we had not reckoned with at all was a child and our misconceptions about caring for it.

To live for a woman and child! Have we reached a point where it is possible for a woman to live for a woman and child? Do I really want to take on the responsibility of a child I did not bear? Do I want to forego being pregnant, giving birth and nursing the child?

If I were to have a child it would be with the full knowledge that I alone would be responsible for it. The experiences of people around me have made it clear that I cannot depend on anything or anyone aside from myself, whether on one man, one woman, a group of people.

I would have to sleep with a man in order to get pregnant. But I would not be capable of going to bed with a man merely for the sake of getting pregnant.

I would have to go back to work full-time in order to support the child. I would have to put it in a daycare center. If I had to work all day earning not much more than five hundred dollars a month—and then take care of the child in the evening—how could I find the time to grow?

My head was two steps ahead of my body. Our commune dissolved. In the city the apartment stands deserted. Not one of the three women really wants to take it upon herself to return and unearth what still lay buried in the rooms we left behind.

Hiding out. Three months. A transition.

Optimism should have been the driving force, new plans should have spurred me on. I was undecided and exhausted. This transitional period suited me fine. My room was tiny, but there was a window over my desk. It looked out onto a quiet courtyard, the sofa bed was a yard wide. Before going to sleep I would put the cassette recorder right up next to the pillow so that I could listen to very soft music, one side of my face pressed up tightly against the silvery speaker.

The nights are my own again. Ideas come to me in the still of night and I have time to pursue them. I have to be sure that no one will disturb me, that I won't meet anyone on the way to the kitchen or bathroom, that the telephone won't ring. At four in the morning I discover the sky. Dawn begins to rise from the edge of the world, the square of light stretched over the four-cornered courtyard grows azure and inflates to a dome. I lean out of the window. How can this pale strip of sky, which I usually notice only when I daydream or feel nostalgic, suddenly turn into an azure dome? My cheeks feel different. I'd like nothing better than to go down and build a fire by the garbage cans and play Rumpelstiltskin.

I can still feel in my bones all the mornings when I had to catch the train at a minute past seven and shortly thereafter start work in my stiffly starched uniform. Does the sky seem so blue just because I am the only one in the whole building who sees it at this time of day? It has been years since I found myself wide awake at four in the morning, energized by my own thoughts. Not on the weekend but in the middle of the week, not at a party, not with someone, but rather alone.

In the buried, bygone years I had been storing things up. Now that I am more alert, in a place with more time and more energy, I can finally piece together my fragmented thoughts.

I study the notes I have made over the past ten years and hesitantly begin to work my way through my past. The focal point of my existence has imperceptibly shifted to my own history and to the discovery of the woman I am now. It happens only rarely that I can write several days in a row. Outside demands are made on me. New groups, new projects require my participation. Though in the back of my mind I ponder how I might better shield myself from too many demands, I nevertheless join in, this desire to take part is an almost automatic response. I make hasty decisions which turn out all wrong, and which are followed by equally rash retractions.

New projects crumble faster than before, structures break down.

I wander back and forth between my exposed history and the dissolving structures surrounding me. I am thrown back on myself again and again. This is my nature. I am beginning to discover my capacity for change.

This has become the most important, most tangible point of departure for everything that lies ahead.

I have planned a trip to America and Mexico. The time is right. Away from it all I will be able to get a better perspective, perhaps even make decisions. In any case, I will learn again what it is to travel.

For three months I have no visitors. Various women's groups meet occasionally in the living room of the apartment. I am not missing anything. But one night, sitting at my desk, I feel uptight. Behind me lie weeks of extreme exertion, weeks filled with preparations, projects, appointments. For the first time in nine months I made a date to meet a man for dinner. In fact, it is the first time in a long while that I spend an entire evening with someone. We talk for hours. We are unencumbered, new to each other. On the street we suddenly embrace, laugh. How simple it is, how automatic.

When I ruled out intercourse, other gestures which we had only as accessories to coitus were also precluded.

Access to women has been blocked off. When we try to find the way to our selves, our hands and feet are shackled. Do I find it more stimulating to appeal to a man than a woman? They have *broken our spirits*. This inadequate term, socialization! This prettifying concept, conditioning.

We can move only if we move towards the opposite sex, and even then only in the choreographed movements they taught us when they broke us to harness. We know how to act within these patterns, no matter how horrible the silence between the sexes may be, no matter how murderous the individual actions, how out of step or dissimilar the needs.

"No," I tell him. "I don't want you to touch me. I want to be able to touch Fenna in our own comfortable, natural way. I've known her longer than I've known you. I know her better than I know you. Why do I feel like I have so many arms and legs when I want to touch her?"

Between Fenna and me was the unspoken agreement that we didn't want to become involved with each other. If we had started making too many demands, had become preoccupied, had started longing for each other, our work would have suffered, and that we didn't want. Hours and hours in which we could paint and write would be lost, were we to really encounter and find out about each other.

But gradually it became impossible to ignore the changes which had taken place in us. It seemed as though I could almost reach out and grasp the affection which we sometimes felt for each other. When we met, we beamed at each other and blushed— without being able to turn our joy into a lasting embrace. I slept fitfully when we shared the same bed, afraid of getting too close to her in my sleep.

When walking we put our arms around each other's shoulders or waist. Once in a while we stroked each other's hair. After women's meetings we parted with a sisterly embrace. We embraced with arms hands shoulders, cheek to cheek. Our lips met briefly in a fleeting kiss, and we laughed again and lightly ran a hand along the side of the other's face as if to indicate how much we would have liked to spend more time together.

We did not hug each other with breasts hips legs in these sisterly embraces. We did not kiss each other on

73

the lips like leftist women and men so spontaneously force themselves to (sometimes it was even more likely that one would kiss the boyfriend of another woman than the woman herself).

We found ourselves in empty space. We didn't want to imitate, we wanted to create new ways and means of behavior drawing on our selves and on the untapped reserves of eroticism lying between us. The expanse of unexplored territory had a stupefying effect.

The memory of old behavior patterns faded ever so slowly. The transition seemed to be at hand.

State of Emergency

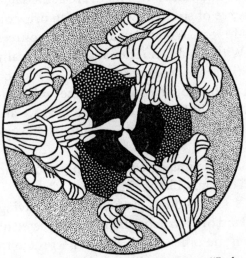

"It is easier for me to talk to women than to men," a woman friend tells me. "It is easier to live with women, easier to get along with them, I feel more comfortable around them than around men . . ."

"But why," I ask her. "Why do you have a relationship with a man, when it is easier for you to *talk, live* and *get along* with women?"

"Approval . . ." she says. "and it is . . . sexual . . . I mean—I haven't had much experience with women, but maybe that was because it wasn't . . . any better than with a man . . ."

"I know what you mean," I say. "Fenna and I had problems too. Not because we wanted men's approval, but because we didn't know how to create a new, unique kind of passion—there is a kind of solidarity between women, one in which compassion, eroticism . . . sincerity and security are wrapped up together. Many of the feelings which often prove disastrous in relationships with men, are at the same time . . . a reserve of strength which we can draw on for mutual support. Women's emotional resources are greater. With a man, emotional atrophy usually sets in so early that somewhere along the way he becomes incapable of having humane relationships . . . he can hold his own only as long as we are there to render him bodily and emotional . . . support . . ."

"But men are victims of conditioning, too!" she interrupts. "You can't blame them for . . ."

"I'm not!" I say. "I don't blame them for having learned that kind of destructive behavior expected of men . . . but on the other hand, I *do* expect them to want to change—but I don't see any sign of that happening . . . not even with men who in terms of their work, life style, intellect would seem capable of changing, not even with men who claim that they would like to shed their masculine skin . . ."

"But they aren't all like that . . . sometimes it is possible to have . . . a humane relationship with a man . . . even sexually . . . a humane sexuality . . ."

"It is possible to have a humane sexual relationship with a woman," I counter.

"Even women try to control each other," she says. "Exclusivity has not been overcome, you still see jealousy, dramatic scenes, calamities . . ."

"It's such an easy way out to say that women haven't got all the answers either," I reply. "It goes back to the idea that women are supposed to be model human beings—simply because they are women . . . It is hard to be humane. When women get together, they are still just groups of human beings who have been deformed by society. They have certain basic things in common—their sex is the color of their skin. They share a common cultural, historical, sexist . . . past and still live in the same sexist society . . . among themselves they can cast off the traditional roles if they really want to—and here, it seems to me, the fundamental issue is one of a woman coming to terms with her self, whether or not she ever slept with another woman is not the important thing . . ."

"I agree," she says. "It is simply not true that it is necessarily better with women . . ."

"You're missing the point," I retort. "First of all it is a question of wanting to *fundamentally* change relationships between people, and this would imply, among other things . . . foregoing traditional relationships which are based on stereotypes. It is a question of woman realizing that she doesn't need another person to feel like a complete human being. But whether or not she will succeed depends upon the kind of work she does, her children, upon all the demands that are made on her—where can she find the strength to break free? The strength to become abnormal? To me it seems more and more unnatural, I really do mean *unnatural*, to have had access only to people of one sex. For the last twenty-six years for example, I had to live without another woman's breast . . . how could I ever have known what it is like to bury my head in someone's breasts? When I am together with another woman I learn something about my self. With a man I learn only that I am different and that my body is supposed to be there for him, I don't really learn about my body or about my self . . ."

"But the electricity, the attraction . . . something is missing . . ."

"Do you mean that which is usually termed 'sexual arousal?'" I ask. "Doesn't anything happen when you're together with a woman? You don't feel anything in the pit of your stomach, you sit across from her, feeling a bit awkward perhaps . . ."

"Exactly," she says. "That's exactly how I feel!"

"Of course," I say, "but that's just it, then why do you still want to sleep with her? You feel this closeness to her, you have finally met up with that which you've always been giving to men, for the first time it is not only you who is paying attention, offering support and compassion, you are, instead, also the recipient, you sense another woman evoking in you a feeling of . . . longing, when up to now only men had found that women evoked feelings of longing in them . . . the man himself cannot evoke longing in you. Isn't it really the case that your sense of longing is the desire to evoke desire in him? . . . It isn't our body we learned to love . . . it is merely the desire that our body arouses in a man . . . do we love the male body or . . . do we love being desired? The period when the male body could evoke longings in us . . . belongs to the past—what is it you are really longing for, when you long for that body?"

"But what about . . . approval . . ." she says hesitantly. "Can you get along without men's approval?"

"What is it they should approve of? Is it important that they accept me, that in their eyes I conform to the image of what a woman should be? In fact it's the eyes that really get to me, I mean literally these eyes which reflect the distorted bodies of women in rightist and leftist magazines. It is this distorted perspective . . . that we are supposed to measure up to, these eyes reduce me to an object . . . and whether or not I feel whole, they dismember me, they focus on my breasts . . . this also happens with friends and acquaintances and not only with strangers on the street. I always get that uncomfortable feeling . . . that a man wants something from me. He invariably demands that I lavish my undivided attention on him as soon as he appears on the scene—because he is a man and I am a woman. He expects me to notice him, to be interested in him because he is a man and I am a woman—for no other reason! He naturally assumes that the woman who is graced with his approving stare is at his disposal . . . I feel less inhibited among women . . ."

"But you are being just as one-sided," she says, "that's not any different . . ."

"But it is," I say, "it *is* different. I admit that it is one-sided, but that's not the issue, what is important to me is whether I am getting hurt, whether I am being weakened or strengthened . . . severed relationships can't be mended from one day to the next! . . . and why should women do that all by themselves? They provide the impetus, men have to take it from there. I cannot, for example, ignore the fact that during all the thousands of years of male domination, the penis, just like all other implements . . . has become a weapon, and the attitude towards everything living has become correspondingly sadistic and destructive. The experiences most women have had with intercourse are ghastly enough without even mentioning abortions and torture."

"Everything has gotten so complicated!" she says. "But it must be possible to find one man somewhere with whom one could have a humane relationship . . . I don't want to exclude him from my life, but I am no longer going to be there just for him alone, women are part of my life too . . ."

"I know, a man sometimes will sit there in the room without budging when he knows damn well that his woman wants to have a private conversation with other women!" We both start to laugh.

"This how-can-you-do-this-to-me look," she says, "because I am no longer there alone next to him! It didn't use to make any difference to him what I did— he had his work, his football buddies, his political group and me—but now that I have a women's group . . . what's going on with him? Sometimes a woman does arouse a new kind of feeling in me, a different kind of attraction . . . one which can, for a few seconds, be so intense that it carries over into the following day. It is also an erotic sensation and it is fulfilling—it is not only the signal of some dubious need for 'more' . . . I used to believe I was content all day after having slept with him, whether or not I had an orgasm, simply because I was with him—but now I feel empty when we sleep with each other, even though I do enjoy it, I do like having sex with him . . . I do get aroused . . ."

"Do you really?" I ask, "or are you saying that only because the idea is so engrained in your mind, and because you can rationalize intercourse that way?

Don't we usually sleep with a man because of social pressures rather than because we . . . feel secure? Don't we often take a man in because that gives us the feeling of being needed. And if copulation is unpleasant or humiliating, we still have ample opportunity to remain somewhat detached—what goes on in the far reaches between penis and vagina doesn't really have to concern us. The penis is too . . . alien to be able to really reach us—this sort of schizophrenia has become incredibly complex and multifaceted! We need it for self-protection—in order to survive . . . we fake enjoyment in order to come up to expectations, in order to be left alone—can you talk to him about sexuality?"

"Hardly!" she says. "He gets scared, feels hurt, has guilt feelings—how am I supposed to tell him that I feel unfulfilled with sleeping with him . . . that I don't feel close to him, that weeks go by when I don't want to go to bed with him . . . perhaps things would improve if the intervals between intercourse were longer, if we would spend more time talking to each other. Can you talk to Fenna? Did you two have sexual problems?"

"Yes," I say. "It took a long time before we felt we could be open with each other, before we could talk about what each of us wanted. Even with her it took a long time before I believed that she actually found my body beautiful. It was of course different, hearing it from her than from a man, but I still didn't trust myself . . . I noticed, too, that with a man, the real sense of touch usually gets lost in the myriad of prescribed stimuli and responses . . ."

"Yes, that's how it seems to me, too. But how does

this new way of touching become ... different and yet exciting?"

"It takes time," I say. "Time played a really important role in building an intimate relationship. Now a new sense of longing, of excitement, of devotion has come into being—but it is devotion which stems from affection rather than from submission and brute force. This male society has gotten under our skin. It takes all the strength we can muster just to keep from perpetuating it, through conditioned gestures, wishes, activities, and reactions ... why, for instance, do you put on makeup when you go out to meet a man, even though you don't wear any at home?"

"I want to look good, want him to find me attractive ..."

"Do you go out to dinner with women too? Do you find that exciting, fascinating, do you look forward to that or does it seem less interesting than going out with a man? Don't women have anything to report about the big wide world out there, do you feel that only men, at least for a moment, can help you overcome the feeling of being closed in?"

"It is true that women's experiences out in the world are limited, but that isn't the problem. I'm more interested in women than in men, their history, their lives are more interesting than men's, it's easier to talk to them. But when we are ready to leave ... even if we walk home together ... I just don't know where to go from there ..."

The winter after my return from America is mild. In December we can go for walks in the gardens of the Charlottenburg Palace. Here and there crocuses are blooming. Fenna and I walk along with our coats unbuttoned. She stops, lifts her face towards the sun and slowly says, I would like to be passionately in love again—I am not really interested in becoming involved, yet I'd like to experience that passion again, with a woman, I want to feel that special excitement as soon as I walk in the door . . . I don't believe we are capable of that anymore.

I nod. Yes, I say, I feel the same way. But I still need time to recuperate. Recovering from the wounds inflicted over the past ten years is taking longer than I thought it would. I have no sexual needs. I want only peace and quiet, time to write. What do we really mean by passion, excitement?

A year ago, shortly before I left for America, the venture with Fenna began to take shape. We came upon regions of human affection which had lain fallow until then. We were not in love at the start, and we warily watched our moves. For a long time we were equipped with nothing but the knowledge that we wanted to have something to do with each other— we even had to learn how to speak. We were at one and the same time helpless and grateful in barren, unmapped territory.

I am quite sure
that you used to dwell in trees
as I in lakes and rivers.
In my glittering hair of moss
solar energy erupted.

Your strands of hair fanned down
along the roots through the ground.

They still store up memories
of life within the mantle of bark
each of the dark tendons
is taut with the strength
of survival in the forest. The gnarls
on the trunks, these too
you have brought along with you.

Your hands coarse and damp
the moment I want to live
with you, not just survive. An unreal
leafy green. You take
refuge in a corner of the blanket
to dry your hands, but also
to keep me out
of your life
and to hide so far away
that only the forest eyes can be seen and
the tiny roots of hair on your forehead.

Life in the water now long past
emerged
onto a barren rock. Surrounded by
perilous swamp, no end
in sight. The rock
no room for two
not yet enough ground broken
for a life outside the water
a bit of mossy hair,
in the sun.

You run lost through the woods, uprooted
hair, most women
long since expelled
or atrophied
crippled and brittle.

84

Only a few broke free
in time.

Many

   individually

           we hatch the world anew
           we stir up time
           we shed our shadow skin
           fire breaks out

I cannot remember anymore,
how many nights there were during that winter
which is almost two years hence, nights when Fenna
and I lay down together in the same bed—back to
back—and warmed each other before curling up to
sleep.

The matter-of-fact way in which we got undressed
and crawled under the covers was comforting.
Perhaps we murmured this or that to each other, lit a
candle or two, when my feet got too cold I warmed
them on her legs before we rolled over and snuggled
up . . . we treated each other kindly and with great
care. The weeks passed peacefully, yet awkwardly.
Since we did not know how to approach each other,
we refrained from touching. Since we did not know
how to view each other's bodies, we refrained from
looking.

In the meantime I had become aware of my need
to throw open my door after finishing my work and

go to Fenna, placing one foot in front of the other as I went. A renewed desire to speak another language after work was done, a new language of skin words, laughing, bubbling billowing sounds had surfaced within me.

I was treading water.

I could not think of any way to get things going between Fenna and me. The sincerity between us was so profound that I couldn't possibly be wily and underhanded. It seemed impossible to break down the reserve that Fenna had displayed when she helped me through my period of withdrawal from sexuality. It seemed that my intimacy with Nadjenka should have made it easier, but there was no comparison. Nadjenka and I were cut from much the same cloth. It was not difficult for us to touch each other. We soon found that we shared a common need, and we could immerse ourselves in it. This was the way it had always been for me. If I didn't feel a certain immediate inexplicable attraction towards the other person, I couldn't make love happen.

This time, though, eroticism developed only gradually. Hesitantly, timorously, it dissipated as soon as we drew back from each other. It lacked vital energy at first.

But there was at least this sense of having the reins in one's own hand for the first time, of not being drawn into a preconceived pattern, of not being led by incomprehensible series of actions and reactions. One had the sense of spinning the threads of one's own fate wittingly.

From time to time we spent a whole day together taking long walks. It was on one of those occasions that we went to Fenna's house afterwards to listen to music. Sitting there, we cuddled up to each other. Our eyes met in agreement, our faces began to draw closer and stopped just before touching. I could submerge myself in the shadowy crescents beneath her eyes. The rim of her iris glimmered green in the last few rays of sun streaming through the window panes. The green emitted light gray beams flecked with amber which converged upon the pupil. The smiling lashes descended slowly and interlaced with those below.

We could hardly draw apart, sighing, laughing, "why haven't we ever . . ."—the obstacles seemed to have been overcome. But as time went on they imposed themselves between us again and again.

Although we went away shortly thereafter and spent a whole week together on a farm, we did not go to bed with each other.

Only the nocturnal hours could have brought us closer, since we were not alone. Besides, Fenna needed the daylight hours for painting. We wanted to make use of the time and peace and quiet and we did not want to neglect our work in favor of sexuality.

Was that really it?

Wasn't it really the fear of losing one's head, the possibility of our lives becoming too entangled, the uncertainty as to whether we were indeed capable of remaining individuals while carrying so much of each other within us?

We vacillated because we had both grown used to being alone, we knew that, in some ways at least, it was simpler to face problems alone.

Piece by piece, dear sister
life by life
fossil by fossil
history by history
fingertip by fingertip
approach by approach
smile by smile
word upon word
skin upon skin
affection upon affection
Oh, sister dear
You'll be amazed at what mountains we build!

Strange things happened that week on the farm. On top of all the difficulties we created for ourselves, there were also external circumstances which kept us from getting together. It did not take much to keep us at a distance.

Just after our lips had taken up from where our last kiss had ended, we were interrupted by cats yowling beneath our window. Our hearts stopped beating, we sat bolt upright in bed. Wasn't that the shadow of a man? Was it really just the wind rustling through the trees? Sobered and wide awake we lay next to each other, apart once again.

"Cats," murmured Fenna, drifting off to sleep, "it would have to be cats that disturb us!"

Another night, as we embraced in spite of suffering from sunburn and chills, we heard a strange, scratching sound behind us: a tiny mouse was sitting on the pillow. One leap and we were both standing in the middle of the room. The mouse disappeared into a hidden crevice. We lay down again and agreed that though we weren't really afraid of mice, we didn't especially like for one to crawl over us. I could not sleep. I kept hearing the scratching every so often, at four in the morning I actually found the mouse sitting next to my head again.

A group of us women had gone together to a vacation spot at the ocean. The castle we were living in was huge, a labyrinthine building with many entranceways.

In the village there was a small old bathhouse, a relic of bygone days. It even had a sauna. We had arranged to meet the old village woman there. Fenna planned to make love to her with all of us there looking on. It was a ritual, no one thought it strange.

The old one was wizened and withered and clothed all in rags. One almost expected her to reek of codliver oil. She hobbled about in shoes made of animal skins. She spoke not a word but was very friendly, serene, she had made her peace with the world.

We sat there in the bathhouse and waited for her to arrive. After she came in, she sat down on the floor and began to take off her stockings, very slowly and ceremoniously. I was sitting next to her. Her heavy gray cotton stockings covered enormously hefty legs bulging with varicose veins. We were awed by her ugliness for we knew that this was what awaited women at the end of their lives. We wanted to rid ourselves of the aesthetic prejudices we still carried within us, wanted to begin to revere the ancient misshapen old ones like her.

It all took too long to suit me, I left. Later on, the

others told me that the ritual had not taken place after all, why, I don't know.

How could Fenna and I overcome our shyness and fear? How were we to learn to touch, kiss, confront the lips between our legs?

Is it this image which shocks people into reacting so defensively when the subject of lesbian love is broached? One allows one's own hand, a man's hand, a penis, a man's mouth to do that which is forbidden between women.

We have learned to kiss the penis, and yet are afraid of the
lips between our own legs.
The hand on its way to the clitoris
of another woman
traverses centuries.
It can get lost a thousand times.
It fights its way through fragments of civilization.
And in addition, the route it takes
leads to a place which has no name:
I have no clitoris.
I have no vagina. No vulva. No pussy.
No bust, no nipples.
My body is corporeal. There are no places on my body which correspond to these incorporeal and brutal designations. Clitoris has nothing in common with this part of my body which is called clitoris. In order to find new words I will have to live differently for as many years as I have lived believing in the meaning of these terms.

This part of my body which is called clitoris is not my focal point, my life does not revolve around it. It

90

is not that I want to minimize its importance, it is just that I do not want to be limited again to only one part of my body.

I am beginning to see myself for what I really am.

I assemble the separate parts to make one whole body. I have breasts and a pelvis.

My legs run together to form curves, folds, lips. I glide and fall with Fenna through meadows of blossoming labella (only a man could have named one of these erotic feminine flowers *snap-dragon*).

From now on we'll just call them vulva-flowers, Fenna decides.

I set the scene: Hello, I'd like a
                    bunch of vulva-flowers . . .
What do you want? Get out of here!
Fenna and I convulse with laughter.

That's not right, I interrupt, having a vulva is nothing to be ashamed of. I take a good look at myself, become immersed in the hues, the shadings, the variegations of skin. The lips of my vulva are wrinkled folds. They really do look like rolled up flower petals, reddish-brown and bright pink when I gently unfurl them. How many different unknown shades of colors to be discovered on my body! We create ourselves anew by touching, looking, talking. My breasts pendulate before her body, they begin to laugh, to vibrate with novel sensations. Gently I place a breast on her eye. How apropos that in German men say "it fits like a fist in the eye" . . .
—It looks nice
                    Um hm, purplish—
—Couldn't you go on any longer?
                    No, I'd lost you—

91

—Yeah, it really is difficult sometimes . . .
Bubbles of laughter fill the room. Genital solemnity, where is your sting?

"I still can't quite deal with our relationship," said Fenna in the last conversation before I left for America. "I can't fit us into my life. I don't even know whether I want to—my painting is still the most important thing to me." I felt rejected. "What we have between us hasn't helped me up to now. I am still afraid of being taken over," she went on.

She was sitting way over on the other side of the bed. I reached over my hand, an emissary.

"Don't," she said. "Don't touch me. I have to talk first."

"We can talk and touch," I countered.

She refused. "I can't do both."

The initial difficulties we encountered in linking one life to the other surfaced again and again. They did not seem to diminish as time passed. They were still able to overpower us. We constantly expressed our doubts as to whether or not we even wanted to let another person become so important to us. We felt too threatened by the possibility that our feelings would lead to uncontrollable passion, pain, peril. Where does one draw that thin line between seeing each other only seldom and remaining total strangers, between intimacy and addiction? Our encounters were few and far between. There always seemed so little for us to build upon. Our trust in each other did not seem to be increasing, nor did our reticence readily wane. At each encounter it took a while to reestablish our ties.

Talking still exhausted me. It was hard labor for me to learn to speak. After two hours I was totally worn out.

We could never take refuge in sexuality, for us it could never serve as a substitute language for things left unsaid, undone, it could never be used to camouflage problems. Being together demanded a great deal of time. Our intimacies were circumspect. In the time it took for us to exchange a single kiss, I would in the past have already had intercourse and found myself standing there fully clothed and ready to depart.

Today I am leaving for America, I said to myself the following morning as I wandered home through the empty streets. I had to laugh. The word America did not mean anything to me. I knew only that I would be away for three months. There was nothing left for me to do in Berlin, nor was I looking to find anything. It was enough to glide naked through space for a time, covered only by Fenna's warm dry lizard-skin.

In Frankfurt I made one last call to Nadjenka. Her voice still echoed in my ears long after I had arrived in New York.

I am worried about you, she says.

Wanting to reassure her, I say, Nothing is going to happen to me.

I always worry about you, she says, you don't need to go to America for that.

I had not seen her for a long time. I saw her at a women's conference in spring but we didn't really have a chance to talk. She had driven in with a friend in order to see me. But I was all involved in special meetings. She caught me on the run between workshops, plenary sessions and discussions with other women, I was terribly busy, I was all wrapped up, I had no time to sit down and have a private chat with her. Politics was the issue of the moment.

Could our conference have any meaning for Nadjenka, any impact on her, on her daughter, her husband, her household, her life in the suburbs?

I felt a pang when I saw her. Why didn't we have any projects in common? Was my work with these women really irrelevant to her life? Why didn't *she* undertake anything? She attempted to laugh on the wing. Her fair hair still fluttered about her face. She stood there next to the woman she had come with, who also had a child. They seemed able to give each other mutual support, they were thinking of going on vacation together.

Her life is changing, I thought.

She will get along without me.

When had I ever offered her help?

Would it really have helped if I had shared my life with her?

I was not willing to take the risk of restructuring my own life, of beginning a new life with her. We had only talked about *her* venturing the new beginning, the leap into the unknown, the break with the past, she was supposed to be the one to finally pull herself together and raze her former dwelling...at that time I had not realized how much I was asking of her. I only saw how uncomplicated my life was in Berlin, how easy it was to make contact with the many groups, I was young, I had time, time enough to ask Nadjenka to come and join me in Berlin.

She felt old and all worn out, thirty, feared the unknown . . . the leftists didn't impress her. How could I, myself a ghetto dweller, have countered her objections? She watched me moving from one commune to the next, running through group after group, humanizing man after man.

Seeing you again at the women's conference was very painful for me, wrote Nadjenka. I got the feeling that we didn't really mean that much to each other any more, that our relationship had lost that special something. Something had come between us. You parcel out your affection equally to everybody—I get my share too, of course, but there is nothing special about it.

Her voice reaches me through the telephone: I'm worried about losing you.

Don't be ridiculous, Nadjenka, how could that possibly happen?

Another woman could make it happen, she says. Only another woman can come between uş. I was never afraid of losing you before, a man was never a threat to what we had.

Not even another woman could break up our relationship, I say. It isn't Fenna that you fear, it is the strength I draw from the women's movement, my close ties to those women, the importance I attach to my work with women . . . I do relate to you differently now than I used to when on the rebound from a man . . . but that doesn't mean that you're not still someone very special to me—no, I repeat, it isn't

Fenna. It is that your life is so different from mine while Fenna's and mine are so alike—both of us are single, neither of us has children, we're both involved with "Bread ♀ Roses" . . . for more than two years we have been helping shape that group and give it new direction.

For months Nadjenka kept me at arm's length, nothing changed until she came to visit me at the beginning of the following year. She didn't want me to be a part of her life anymore, she shut me out only to take me back in again, she weighed the situation, pondered. She tried to examine the strands of her life, tried to untangle those hard knotted strands. I didn't hear from her all the while I was gone, she doggedly remained silent.

"There were times when I really missed you while you were in America," said Fenna as we walked through the gardens of the Charlottenburg Palace. "I can't tell you exactly what it was, but it seemed to be more difficult to cope with things. Conflicts were harder to resolve, once when I had my period I just broke down—not that I necessarily wanted to spend more time with you, it was more . . . the idea that I could discuss my problems with you . . . I longed for your . . . emotional support."

The summer had passed us by. The warmth would have favored our attempts to get together, I thought. Now we will have to bundle ourselves up again in two or three layers of clothes, coats caps scarves and gloves.

Brussels, a telephone booth. My head spinning,

the first thing I did upon arriving was to change some money.

Hello? Fenna's voice on the other end.

It's me, I finally say.

Veruschka! Where are you?

In Brussels.

If I leave right away, she says slowly, I can meet you in Frankfurt and we can still drive back tonight.

I steady myself on the wall of the phone booth. You mean you're really going to come pick me up?

She laughs. What do you think I meant?

"This bond between us . . ." I said, as we continued our walk through the gardens, "I think it has something to do with that nebulous notion of 'motherliness.' That term is so ambivalent, so ambiguous . . . how can we attain immediate, direct access to 'motherliness?' For too long we have been thought of as nothing but furrows for sowing seeds—the issue here isn't . . . the woman who gave birth to each of us . . . it's not the blood ties, the guilt feelings, the silence that we want, it . . . isn't a question of making amends, of 'motherliness' only towards her, the issue is the power of motherliness, motherliness as a shared human characteristic . . ."

Two days before Easter it is snowing, sodden and ugly. When I had taken a walk in the park at Christmas, the forsythia were blooming.

I curse as I put on my heavy winter coat, hurry to the subway and immerse myself in a book. I'm *already* snowed in, lost to the world. Last night I was taught to swim like a fish, to cleave through the waters, to part the seas, to furrow them. Mightier than the oceans!

After treating my private patient I return to the apartment, swearing a blue streak. Some nice soup will come to my rescue, you can always depend on cauliflower. I wash the dishes in order to warm my hands. I would like nothing better than to refill the sink with fresh hot water for each and every dish.

My head, charged with bolts of lightning from the ride on the subway, is ready to burst, the soup is steaming next to the typewriter, it tastes like cardboard and like the gray walls in front of my window, its warmth only skin deep. Soon there will be ice water flowing through my veins. I take refuge in the kitchen, turn on all three gas burners and let the blue flames flare; I want to put on some water for tea, pour it into me by the gallon until I am thawed out. I let the laundry run through the machine two, three, five, ten times, hotter than blazes!

The washing machine is sizzling, the plastic is melting, the kitchen is steaming, my hair is standing on end, my head explodes. Cold sweat, with clammy fingers I turn off the gas flames, the washing machine.

I'm getting my period.

The uterus lies cramped between the pelvic bones. The lining of the inner walls is saturated with blood. Dark brown spots for three days now, traces of bright red on the tampon. The lining stubbornly refuses to detach itself. It is taking unusually long this time, it's a nuisance. My head is spinning and this waiting

98

weighs upon me like oppressive weather. The skin on my abdomen is more taut than usual, stretched tightly over the contracting uterus, the pelvic musculature has become too tense, it tugs downward. In previous months the pain had been sudden and acute. Almost the whole lining had been expelled the first day, dark clots. But immediate relief had followed, my tummy warm and relaxed, a premonition of what a period could be like.

Nadjenka came to see me. It can only have been two weeks ago, yet it seems as if she has been gone forever. The long weekend was much too short; afterwards I was filled with an emptiness as never before, I could hardly warm up again. At night her life preyed upon me, tore at my breast.

The pain radiating, sometimes I have to stop in my tracks. To have your period on the weekend, of all times, the two days without interruption from the outside world. Monday is shot, private patients in the morning, and the afternoon spent at the clinic where I work part time. Just looking at the typewriter gives me a backache. (My back is killing me, says a patient, I have the curse.) The muscles contract again and again in order to loosen the lining. Nadjenka's spasmodic sobs still cling to me, she is choking, her life is strangling her. I rock her gently, tell me what's wrong . . .

Never had a choice. Became a secretary because there was no money for anything else, married to get away from home, to finally have a home, had a child, after many years finally a child, in order to . . .

"What'll happen to you, if anything happens to her?"

Nadjenka becomes faceless. Impossible to imagine. "It's simple," she says then, slowly. "Either I'll go on living without her or I won't."

"Perhaps."

What a burden for a mother to bear, right from the very moment of conception, this anticipation of being abandoned. Is life to be reduced to the attempt to overcome loneliness?

"Berlin wouldn't have been the answer, I know that for sure now," she says. "I needed someone to take me by the hand, and you couldn't have done that. You can't imagine the shape I would have been in, how dependent I would have been on you, at least for quite some time."

Each of us had had a man at our side at that time, later our lives took decidedly different courses. Perhaps our getting together would have destroyed everything?

She is my alter ego. When I encounter her, I encounter a part of my self as well. No shared projects, outside interests, hardly a common history. Yet the intimacy lingers, no matter how seldom we see each other. If we were together, would we discover that much was lacking? Is this intimacy really a basis or is it ultimately only that which we cannot—or only with great difficulty—achieve with other people. Someone approaches me the same way I approach others—does that make her my alter ego, is Nadjenka a mirror image, or are we mistaken, but if so, about what . . . why shouldn't we believe each other, why shouldn't we be able to shelter each other, be close to each other despite spatial distance?

Perhaps my period is all loused up this time, maybe everything is blocked up. I get the speculum and take a look. The mouth of the cervix appears from the depths, stands out glistening, brilliant between the coral walls enclosing it.

Out of the circular opening a drop of bright red blood, more of them gather, run down from the vault of the cervix, the confluence of the red river. I can't help smiling, the flashlight illuminates more than the cervix. The darkness of the past fifteen years pales. For fifteen years, every month, red days. I have *my* period, it belongs to me. Having my period was my only chance to belong to my self.

I remember back to the days in school when the girls who were menstruating had to bring a note from their mothers to be excused from gym. Each girl was terribly proud the first time she could present this note, it made her a member of the secret society, it gave her a certain feeling of power. Once in a while, just for the fun of it, all of us would appear before the gym teacher with forged excuses, disconcerted, he would mutter: But—you can't—all—at the same time . . . how could he prove the contrary? So we were free to leave, as soon as he came, we took off. Menstruation was a collective event. The cramps, clenched teeth during class, fleeting conversations in the bathroom—all of that met with an understanding smile, a knowing glance.

The traces on the tampon are bright red for one more day. But then the cramps grow stronger, they radiate out from the uterus, I get diarrhea. I lie down, toss and turn trying in vain to find a comfortable position. The warmth from the heating pad finally seems to help a bit, I drink hot tea with milk. It still hurts, I curl up into a ball, anything to keep from having to straighten my back now. The blood is rushing through my head as usual, I am sweating, all at once saliva collects in my mouth and I try to fight it off but finally stumble to the toilet and spit up the tea. My face is blotchy and contorted. I lie down again, it seems to have passed. Another day is ruined, perhaps by evening I'll be able to think clearly again.

State of Emergency

A woman travels through Germany
ten bleak hours through the chill of night.
Already at the signal of departure
her face shatters
penned in among the sultry vapors of the moving train
she rebels
to avoid being crushed by that fragment of life
at her disposal

Myself outside
before the icy window pane
my breasts sway
anxiously to and fro
a long night coming as the train rushes on
from the fibers of my lips
grow incredulous blossoms

into her abandonment. How far removed
from me she rests
with the deep folds between her legs
from which she brought forth
a daughter, to avoid remaining
alone in that fragment of life
at her disposal.

At the first light of dawn
my anxious breasts must yield.
Lost blossoms wander to and fro
unfathomable between us
to and fro.

Now the red stream is flowing strong, one tampon
can dam it for no more than two hours. My breasts
don't hurt anymore, but the web of veins is bluer than
usual. I am restless, overwrought, I sleep fitfully, am
worn out when I get up, by hand I write words and
lines which I constantly rearrange. In the afternoon I
get tired and try to sleep for an hour. The merry-go-
round inside my head keeps me cold and tense, my
body remains suspended an inch above the bed, only
gradually does it yield, sinking, the pillow meets me
halfway, I can finally rest my head. The cries of the
children playing in the yard fade away, their ball rolls
out of earshot. My toes make my stockings cold. I
glide into darker interstages, the walls of the room
disappear. My racing heartbeat brings me back, I
bury my head in the sleep-enticing folds of the pillow, but it's no use.

At night I walk with other women along a southern
coast. The cliff drops sharply to the dark blue tur-
quoise-mottled sea below. We have to fight our way
against a wall of wind, but while the others move on
forward, I am caught up in a funneling draft of air
and slung in spirals towards the sky. Flying! I spread
my arms. Above me an incandescent seagull floating
with me in the same ethereal stream. In gentle waves
we glide through the luminous heavens.

This year I had enough time to spend five weeks in the north of Germany. My need for space, for room to breathe, was satisfied in a new way, space gave way to other space. The unsettling vastness of far-away places, the disquieting expanse of foreign lands, the stimulating space of the cities—all these needs were not yet satisfied, yet I did not long for those other places.

Vastness

in which the sun still shone brightly, pouring its balmy light across the sky. The yarrow growing wild at the bottom of the field was so high that I disappeared in it whenever I waded towards the fence to gaze across the meadow. High above in the blue streaked with white, an airplane left its trail every evening at the same time. Oddly enough, I didn't sense the usual pang of take-me-along.

Sitting there behind the house and watching the sinking sun I began to remember that about two years ago this longing for trees, sky, space had last surfaced in me. But since then I hadn't been aware of it or if it had arisen for a moment, I hadn't taken it seriously. It was two years ago, when returning from a trip to Switzerland after spring vacation and landing at the airport in Berlin, that I noticed that the exhilaration of being home was missing. That hadn't happened in five years. Even on the long bus ride home, the usual excitement of being home again was absent. I knew where I was, swayed nonchalantly past familiar buildings and shop windows. I must be exhausted, I decided. I have to get up at six tomorrow, there won't be any time to think until the weekend.

When I reached the apartment I was sharing with the other women, I landed right in the middle of a group meeting. I felt a strong sense of aversion. The naked bulb hanging down in the living room burned brightly, inhospitable as always; I could only make out the silhouettes of the various women. I wanted peace and quiet, wanted to be home at last. Something was pulsating in my head, dark green shadows. The floodwaters of the Aare River, which had impressed me so, rose inside me for a moment as I put down my bags in my dark room. The walks along the lush overgrown banks, pleasantly light and sunny— I'd done nothing but take walks and look around.

Hours later, when I slipped between the smooth sheets, the green shadows of the darkness began to grow, they overran my bed, a rustling filled the room: There were forests, whole forest regions reflected in the train windows from Bern to Zurich.

I'm getting old, I thought to myself that night on the farm as I drifted off to sleep. At least the landscape of Switzerland doesn't disturb me any more.

I am a slow brooder. I walk around for days without finding any words, or can't choose between the words I do find. They are all inadequate. It wouldn't be so bad if all I had to do was choose the words and then arrange them in a certain order, construct the phrases and arrange them in a certain pattern, and, having done this, find that everything I wanted to say would be there in black and white. But I must create new words, must be selective, write differently, use concepts in a different way. Every so often a word breaks out of my walled-in brain. In the morning I often awaken in the middle of a sentence, at night, agitated, I jump out of my warm nest, a word, an image, paper, pencil! Quick, before the landslide in my head begins, before I can clack away at the typewriter until my arms fall off. I let them lie there. The skin on my forehead is cool from the beads of icy sweat. I am full and empty.

There is lightning in the courtyard. The stagnant heat has paralyzed me for days. With arms folded I stand at my window. If only it would start to pour. The bleak light tries to peel away the heat from the walls of the building, but it tenaciously refuses to yield. Across the adjoining parking lot bits of paper whirl about in the breeze. An arid wind begins to blow between the buildings, the gusts becoming stronger and stronger.

The light reminds me of the fallow horses Fenna and I had once seen in the country, the tiny foals nestling up against the bellies of the mares.

A door slams shut. I leave the window and walk through the almost empty apartment. Three of the women have gone on vacation. The wind has already scattered the papers lying about on their desks. Will I be able to breathe more freely in this apartment after the storm has blown over? Ever since I came back from the farm it has seemed stifling and cramped in here.

"I figured you would probably come back feeling somewhat alienated and out of touch," said a woman I live with.

I close the windows. The high ceilings, the walls, everything is closing in on me. I feel like a mummy in this setting. I'd like to empty all six rooms with one fell swoop, throw open all the doors and windows. How could I ever have thought this apartment so large? I take all the pictures down from the walls of my room. Fenna brings me her painted clouds of the north German sky.

The light has turned sulfurous. The room grows dim, the wind has done its job. Now the rain begins to trickle down.

I stretch my hands out of the window. How they were filled with Fenna's full lush lips. They floated through my fingers. My hands a chalice, I search for imprints left behind, but only a calyx of fragrance remains.

Just now in the bathroom
I wanted to take a cold shower because I
felt faint
I noticed that I still
am a bit tan at least
the skin tone on my shoulders and neck
is different than
where my breasts begin
Fenna! and I write you a letter since I wonder
when you'll ever have the time and chance
to observe,
at length and in detail
as such observation demands, that
the skin tone on my shoulders and neck
is different than
where my breasts begin?

                    We constantly
                                come up against
limits in our explorations. The limits
of our own strength of available time of
economic resources, of our careers and
our longings. When can we
clarify what longings really are? How can we make
room for our sensual life? The new
emerges but slowly, shedding the old, patchwork.

Do you know this feeling in your abdomen
when the uterus for no apparent reason
contracts and sensations arise out of
fear of being tested, out of sexual desire and
menstrual pain? For years this feeling has now and
again surfaced even when I was under no
extraordinary pressures in the middle of the day
perhaps without apparent cause.

But if I think of
how I felt in the kitchen as a child,
I can retrace the faint trail—
relationships which have been severed
or damaged beyond repair.

    Last night in my dreams I stood before a three-
paneled mirror. When I looked straight in I saw my
face as it looks back at me during the day or in recent
photos, only my hair was still long and piled atop my
head. When I turned my head to the left my face
changed in that side of the mirror, it was my eyes
which were first transformed. Bruises appeared all
around my eyes, dark blue on my eyelids purplish

along my cheekbones. My eyebrows became bushy
and black my skin wilted. My hair turned gray and
coarse.

It did not surprise me that my face had aged.

But it became the face of a total stranger. Not a
single line was familiar. If I turned straight ahead
again I saw my real face. So the old woman in the left
half of the mirror must have something to do with
me. I was startled because the face seemed disfigured
and I moved closer to get a better look at the bruises.
I discovered a delicate pattern of veins in the purplish marks. I turned sideways to the left portion of
the mirror and looked at my shoulders, then my
back. A shawl was draped across my shoulders: a veil
of twining tendrils and flowers green blue and red.
From above the aged face peered down at me. Fenna,
I said, look, look how beautiful that is!
What's going on here? My face ages on my
body a new fabric. I finally realize
that I always thought my body unfashionable
out-of-date, and that thinking it
out-of-date actually spared me much.
If I hadn't complicated matters so much
carrying my body around a dead weight,
if I hadn't lugged it around as I did
I would have been more completely co-opted by
everyday sexuality. My body itself kept that from
happening. It didn't measure up to
male expectations.
I can recognize fragments of my own past history
as well as that of all other women.
There is a trend which gives direction
to the future even in the present

there are multiple layers of processes going on at
different speeds rhythms and on
different levels.
There is no simultaneity to be found. The various
processes collide inside of me
at different points in time with varying degrees
of impact—this sense that life is sometimes
so *compacted*. Even though it is already a
thing of the past I often think of
what I felt on the flight back from New York.
I knelt on the floor and pressed my face against
the window as the plane took off. Far below
the coast disappeared, a white outline. When I
saw that it actually resembled the one
on the globe I had a fleeting image of
America and an idea of the contours of the globe
as a whole. Again I felt this urgent desire to
lnow the *world* as I flew back to Europe, back to
Berlin without knowing what I was still seeking there.
But in these last glimpses of the American coastline
I had a certain feeling, one which flared up only to
die down again, a feeling that I was not really
returning but rather moving on without ever
taking hold.
How casually this giant continent
coasts into the ocean!
It gave me such a lift, seemed so simple and
natural seeing it, the confines of my own body
could expand for a few moments.
Our being, on the other hand, is
boxed in on all sides.
Now that it seems that we are not smothering

each other even though the intimacy has grown
now that the perils of a love affair
while not completely ruled out
have so far at least been held in check . . .
now we notice that we can't do anything right.
A long time ago
we began with the vague desire
to have something to *do* with one another. Now that
it is really a serious matter, we find there are
so many obstacles to overcome. We must constantly
neglect something in favor of something else.
The job suffers because of political activities the
political activities because of the job
the job on the other hand doesn't bring in
enough money earning money takes time away from
our other important work.
We lose each other along the way. Constantly having
to decide
between us and our work—that too a
conflict—if we neglected our work the perils
of a love affair would mount. Painting and
writing to some extent offer tangible guidelines,
it is only because of these that we can survive,
that we can attempt to transcend
the tragically restrictive means of communication
open to us.
But we cannot rise above the fits of anger and
despair.
Tomorrow morning I will ring your doorbell you
will open the latch I will drop these pages into
your mailbox, having compressed into a few lines
that which would require many hours

111

not perhaps to capture
our longings but to communicate them
not perhaps to live but to suspend
merely surviving
for a few hours.

Gourd Woman

It was already a little after eight-thirty.

Cloe got up in a daze. As she ran down the long hall to the telephone her breasts ached; she cradled them protectively in her hands. When she sat down and picked up the receiver she felt a twinge in her ovaries. Had another four weeks gone by?

Six or seven periods ago her breasts had started hurting a few days before menstruation, especially when she ran. Ever since she had begun loving her breasts, life had come into them; hence, pain as well.

After finishing the conversation she put the receiver back on the hook and walked slowly into the bathroom. When she looked up into the mirror, still bending over the wash basin, shaking the water from her face and reaching for the towel, she couldn't help but smile. In the mirror, two soft pale brown gourds nodded towards the basin. In the country sunshine fine white hairs had become visible. Cloe laughed aloud. Porcupine breasts! she murmured. Gourd-porcupine, porcupine-gourd . . . She thought of the forbidden oval and round shapes. The womb, a ripened gourd, entrance to the vault, dwelling of the mouth of the womb, an oval shape . . .

She had slept poorly.

These past weeks she'd been totally out of touch. She didn't know whether to look first to the right or to the left when crossing the street; she would stand on the corner until the green light finally turned red and only then start across. Twice already it had happened that she couldn't unlock the door to the building at night because she had been turning the key the wrong way. If footsteps approached her room she would draw her shoulder blades together in fright and hold her breath—hoping no one wanted to come in. It was almost impossible for her to walk through the living room if someone was sitting in there. She felt hemmed in by expectations of a glance, recognition, a conversation.

She listened to music when she needed to take a break from writing. She was no longer capable of relating to anyone during these intervals. Sometimes she would have liked nothing better than to sit down on the kitchen floor in front of the washing machine and spend hours staring at the colored laundry that tumbled to and fro.

Cloe turned off the water and plunged her face into the towel. The skin on her face was beginning to get bumpy again, it had started on the way back from the farm. Along her lower jaw, just in front of her ear, a white spot had suddenly erupted and begun to itch and swell. —Nono, I'm sure nothing stung me, this just happens sometimes. Now they had started appearing one after the other in the course of the day, occasionally a new one would be there when she woke up. From time to time the skin would prickle a l over her body, grow taut, stretched too tightly around her, protesting against clothing, noise, dirt, sweat and confrontations with people. Sometimes Cloe's skin would not relax until, naked, she slid between the covers and turned off the lights. She was worn and frazzled to the breaking point. She fervently envied people who could lie down *and fall asleep*. Most of all she envied people who could lie down to sleep *because* or *when* they were exhausted. Were she to lie down now, her eyelids would refuse to grow heavy. She would circle behind them, a bundle of gray fluff trying in vain to sink into the listless somnolent expanse above which she floated.

She put on her long dress and, in someone else's slippers that were too large for her, shuffled into the kitchen to heat water for tea. Then she fished the turquoise-colored mug out of the dirty dishes and began to wash it. What urgent little details *life* consists of! The shawl of morning sunlight about her shoulders almost seemed more than she deserved. Hadn't she yet learned to accept what was her due?

Cloe put her hands down; the warm water from the faucet kept flowing over her hands. The scrub brush slid out of one hand, the mug dangled from the other. Lost in thought, she gazed out the window.

115

Warmth suddenly seemed to be the most important thing in life. The warmth of the sun.

From now on I will think in light years, she said aloud, and then quickly looked around, startled. But she was alone in the kitchen. Today was one of those days when layers of dreams, fragments of conversations that she'd had or read somewhere, half-forgotten encounters all hovered in the air like particles of soot after a great fire.

Cloe scrubbed the mug vigorously and set it on the table. I have to clarify where I'm *at*, she thought. No, first I have to figure out *how I got to* this point. I don't know how all these things get into my head. Ever since I've been working and living differently, thoughts and images have been crowding my mind. Not only do I need to get this stuff out of my head, I also have to recollect when and how it got in there, and it is precisely *that* which cannot be put into words. By the time the impressions and thoughts are roaming around inside me and I have started wondering how they entered my mind, they are already distorted. I must guide them into my head so that I can express them in familiar signs, so that others will be able to understand them. These numerous processes of assimilation and alienation must evolve in such a way that the signals emerging from my head and going into the typewriter correspond as closely as possible to the *original* experience, though in another form . . .

The water was boiling. Whenever Cloe showed something she had written to anyone it was already obsolete by the time she got around to discussing it. The words and their sequence were constantly changing in her head. She had to put a stop to that. She didn't believe the claim that a book was "finished" only when each printed sentence could be expressed in one way and no other. A book a process a piece of life, Cloe said to herself—all *change*able.

She took the box of tea down from the shelf, shook a handful of black leaves into the tea strainer, poured some boiling water over it and let the tea steep for a few moments. As she held the tea kettle with her right hand waiting to pour the rest of the water into the pot, she again felt the piercing pressure on the inner edge of her shoulder blade. Sometimes while driving she had hardly been able to lift her arm when she wanted to turn on the radio. Unpleasant sensations radiated from this spot, as though all the muscles, sinews and nerves above and below the shoulder blade were twisted and sprained.

Lately it seemed so senseless to discuss the book with anyone. People's comments only added more rings of emptiness to the ones already encircling her. Her narrative sources had grown silent. Lately there came hardly a clue from the things she was working on, even from the letters themselves there emanated an unsuspected coldness now and then. Frozen solid they surrounded her.

Cloe lifted the strainer out of the pot and emptied it into the garbage bag. She poured herself some tea, sat down at the table and warmed her hands around the steaming mug. I think I'll dye my hair today, she decided. It was consoling to think of the greenish goo working by itself while she pored over the manuscript, so that after two hours her hair would shimmer reddish gold. A year ago she'd had her hair

117

clipped very short. She had wanted to see the shape of her head again and the contours of her face—and she had hoped that with short hair she would not be accosted on the street as often. Her hair had grown in quickly, stronger and fuller. She already had to brush it out of her eyes. She imagined the woman she had been a year ago, and the woman the year before that and . . .

Shedding.

This is the year of the gourd woman! She got up and went into her room. No longer the year of the would-like-to-be-slender woman, the wish-I-were-flat-chested woman . . . Cloe bears traces of her old skins. She is dappled, and walks giggling through the streets. Here and there, in the play of light and shadow, the variegated patches glow. The soft, ready-to-yield skin, the don't-be-so-oversensitive skin, the I-am-tranquility-personified skin, the sensual-curious skin, the want-to-experience-everything skin. Who can read a dappled skin?

Cloe moves her lips. I am my own woman. People turn and stare. To think that nowadays even young women have started talking to themselves!